DEMCO

OUR CHILDREN
SHOULD BE WORKING

OUR CHILDREN SHOULD BE WORKING

By

WILLIAM N. STEPHENS

Professor of Sociology
Dalhousie University
Halifax, Nova Scotia

CHARLES C THOMAS • PUBLISHER
Springfield · Illinois · U.S.A.

Published and Distributed Throughout the World by

CHARLES C THOMAS ● PUBLISHER

Bannerstone House

301-327 East Lawrence Avenue, Springfield, Illinois, U.S.A.

© *1979, by* CHARLES C THOMAS ● PUBLISHER

ISBN 0-398-03851-1

Library of Congress Catalog Card Number: 78-11606

With THOMAS BOOKS *careful attention is given to all details of
manufacturing and design. It is the Publisher's desire to present books that
are satisfactory as to their physical qualities and artistic possibilities and
appropriate for their particular use.* THOMAS BOOKS *will be true to those
laws of quality that assure a good name and good will.*

Printed in the United States of America
V-R-1

Library of Congress Cataloging in Publication Data

Stephens, William N
    Our children should be working.

    Includes index.
    1. Children--Management--Addresses, essays, lectures.
2. Helping behavior--Case studies. 3. Apprentices--
Case studies. 4. Work--Case studies. 5. Child
development--Addresses, essays, lectures. I. Title.
HQ772.S69   649'.1   78-11606
ISBN 0-398-03851-1

ACKNOWLEDGMENTS

I WISH to thank the families who let me come into their homes to observe and the other people who told me their work histories.

The research was funded by a grant from the Strategic Planning and Research Division of the Department of Manpower and Immigration, in Canada. Thanks are due to that agency, and especially to Larry Motuz, the officer in charge of the grant. However, the opinions expressed in this book are my own; they are not necessarily those of the Department.

My research assistants were Laura Chapman and Martha Moeller. Both of them gave me valuable help.

The time I spent doing the research and then writing the book was underwritten by Dalhousie University and by the Canada Council. The book was written on a sabbatical year spent at Florida State University, on a Canada Council leave fellowship. I wish to acknowledge the hospitality I received from the Anthropology Department at Florida State; I especially want to thank Tony Paredes, the chairman, and Lou Causseaux, the secretary of the Department.

A number of people read the manuscript and gave suggestions. I particularly want to thank Phil Martin, Director of University Presses of Florida, for his advice.

Thanks are due to the following for permission to publish quotations from other books:

Margaret Mead, for permission to quote from *Coming of Age in Samoa*, 1928, William Morrow and Company, New York.

Yale University Press, for permission to quote from Leo Simmons' *Sun Chief*.

Harvard University Press, for permission to quote from Beatrice and John Whiting's *Children of Six Cultures*. (1975).

The American Anthropological Association, for permission to quote from the Whitings' "Altruism and Egosim in Six Cultures," reproduced by permission of the American Anthropological Association from *Cultural Illness and Health* (Anthropological Studies #9), p. 60, 1973.

Karl Heider, for permission to quote from his *The Dani of West Irian* (1972).

Quotations from *Changing Children's Behavior*, by John D. Krumboltz and Helen Brandhorst Krumboltz, © 1972, pp. xi-xiv, 48, 54, 62, 121, 177, are reprinted by permission of Prentice-Hall, Inc., Englewood Cliffs, New Jersey.

Quotations from *Problems of Parents* by Dr. Benjamin Spock, © 1962 by Henry Cooper, Trustee, are reprinted by permission of Houghton Mifflin Company.

W.N.S.

CONTENTS

PART II
HOW CHILDREN'S WORK STYLES DEVELOP

PART III
NEW AVENUES OF DEVELOPMENT THAT
HAVE OPENED UP IN OUR SOCIETY

OUR CHILDREN
SHOULD BE WORKING

Chapter 1

INTRODUCTION

Velma nags her twelve-year-old, Betty Lou: "Pick up your things." "Straighten your room." Sometimes Betty Lou picks up her things and straightens her room, but most of the time she does not.

Betty Lou knows how to wash the dishes, do some cooking, operate the vacuum cleaner, and do housekeeping. Occasionally she helps, but Velma does not count on her.

Betty Lou's older sister was also idle around the house. Velma rarely got any real help from either of her daughters: The older sister was always so busy with homework and school projects that Velma did not have the heart to demand housework from her.

Velma had been a hardworking farm girl who grew up during the Great Depression. Both her parents had been sickly, so there were long periods of time when the burden of the farm work fell on her. Velma shakes her head at the hardships she endured. She does not want her children to "know work like that."

THE Nova Scotia farm where Velma grew up represents a bygone age, before modern conveniences, when families were larger. People from that era speak of how hard they worked and how little they expected. In that vanished time, children and teenagers worked alongside adults. They did farm work and helped out within the home. They took paying jobs at an early age.

Modern children have fewer work opportunities. Not so many people live on farms. In modernized homes, there are fewer chores to do. It is even hard to get part-time jobs; the legal working age has been pushed back by child labor legislation and by safety laws.

More and more, children and youth are kept away from the grown-up world of work, and they help out less within the home. This is one reason for modern youth problems — alienation of the young, irresponsibility, and conflict between teenagers and their parents — in the opinion of some sociologists and psychologists.[1]

Betty Lou represents the new generation: living in a modernized home where her help is not urgently needed, with no younger brothers and sisters for which to care. Betty Lou is lazy around the house because Velma did not train her to be helpful. For all her complaints, the fault is still Velma's. However, it should be said in Velma's defense that her household situation is not conducive to training Betty Lou to be helpful. The farm where Velma grew up *was* conducive.

Some modern children still have to work. In large families, on farms, and in certain other homes, children's help is still needed.

> Ursula is seven years old. She is third oldest of five daughters. These girls have been helping out from the time they were very small. The children came so fast that their parents — out of necessity — pressed them into service. The older girls take care of their baby sisters and do other work around the house.
>
> Ursie is especially keen to help her father. She follows him around, observes what he does when he is working on something, and joins in whenever he lets her. A part of one day:
>
> We drive up to a gas station in the family car. Ursie leaps out of the car, grabs a window-washing squeegee, and starts washing the windshield. We shop at a supermarket. Ursie observes with interest, watches quietly. (That is all she can do in that particular setting.) At home again, she watches fascinated as her father prepares a mousetrap. Later she entertains her baby sister, and she helps her older sisters prepare supper.

Children who grow up this way tend to be helpful and maternal. They seem to learn responsibility at an early age. They also get work training that should be useful in later life; they

---

[1]Urie Bronfenbrenner, "The Origins of Alienation," *Scientific American*, August, *231*, No. 2:53-61, 1974.

James S. Coleman et al., *Youth: Transition to Adulthood. Report of the Panel on Youth of the President's Science Advisory Committee* (Washington, D.C., U.S. Government Printing Office, June, 1973), pp. 130-137.

learn skills such as cooking and child care.

What about children who do not grow up like Ursula and Velma? Is there any substitute for farm work and large-family upbringing? Some mothers still train their children to be helpers, even though they do not live on farms or have large families; but they are exceptional.

I have been studying children who work. I have visited large families like Ursie's, lived on farms, and observed various settings in which children and teenagers were working. I talked to parents. I have also taken down the childhood histories of college students and older persons. I even included some children like Betty Lou, who do not work. Most of these people lived in Nova Scotia. The college students were generally my students at Dalhousie University. I gathered some cases in the United States and in Ontario and New Brunswick.

I also included hobbies in my inquiry, and paid jobs that teenagers take, volunteer work they do, hitchhiking, and on-their-own adventuring. To some extent, these fill the gap left by the disappearance of traditional children's work.

Of the two hundred children and young people I studied, the most admirable could be put in four different types.

Helpers like Ursie represent one type. A second type is "mechanical" boys. They usually get their start doing mechanical work at home. They go on to various hobbies. A third type is teenage managers and officeholders. The fourth and most impressive of all is the enterprisers.

Enterprise, office holding, mechanical hobbies — these represent modern-day avenues of development for young people. If a parent cannot train her child to be helpful, perhaps she can start the child on one of these other routes. However:

• Enterprisers, managers, and serious hobbyists represent an elite. Most youth do not develop this way.

• Helping out in the home is the way most of these teenage careers started. The enterprisers, managers, and hobbyists usually worked at home when they were children; this seems to have been the foundation for their later careers.

• Helping out at home provides a distinctive kind of training. The other ways of developing do not fully take its place. However all four of the types — helpers, enterprisers, managers, serious hobbyists — are very impressive. If a child takes any one of these four routes his parents can be proud.

Part I
Helping Out in the Home

Chapter 2

HOW HELPING SHAPES CHARACTER

The young boys constantly watch the occupations of the elder men. In this way they acquire the necessary skill in the same occupations, above all in fishing and hunting. When the Toba boy is about six or seven years old, his father makes him a small bow and arrows with which he frequently practices shooting, thus at an early age acquiring dexterity in managing the weapon. Similarly the girls follow their mothers everywhere, down to the river, to the fields, and the forest, keenly watching how she does her work and soon learning to do the same.[1]

Learning to work was like play.[2]

CHILDREN'S WORK IN PRIMITIVE VILLAGES

THROUGHOUT human history, most people lived close to the land — in peasant villages and in primitive societies, and on unmechanized farms. Much basic work had to be done: People carried in their firewood and water, tended their animals, worked in the garden, hunted, and gathered wild foods. Cooking and getting foodstuffs ready to cook required much work. There was also housework: tending the fire, cleaning up, and maintaining the house. Children's labor was needed. Even small children were put to work on simple jobs. They could run errands, fetch and carry, and help out in small ways. Older children baby-sat and cared for the animals. As they grew older, they were given increasingly more grown-up work to do.

[1]Rafael Karsten, *Indian Tribes of the Argentine and Bolivian Chaco: Ethnological Studies* (Helsingfors, Finland, Akademische Buchhandlung, 1932), p. 10.
[2]Leo Simmons, *Sun Chief* (New Haven, Connecticut, Yale University Press, 1942), p. 25.

Children went through a natural sequence, learning to work. They started as spectators. They imitated adults' work in their play (playing dolls, playing house, playing cook and farmer and herdsman and hunter). Then they were allowed to join in and help. Some time between the ages of three and six, the work-apprenticeship usually began. By puberty, children's work was usually similar to adults'.[3]

The early apprenticeship took advantage of young children's eagerness to be in on what the grown-ups were doing and to imitate what the grown-ups did. First they watched and played at it; then, bit by bit, they were allowed to do real work. The Hopi autobiographer, Don Talayesva, remarked that learning to work was like play. Children were always around when anything was going on in the Hopi pueblo. They were always underfoot, wanting to see what was happening and wanting to participate. So the adults let them participate; before they knew it, they were working.[4]

This seems the ideal arrangement for role modeling — learning and practicing one's future adult role, modeling oneself after some older person. Little girls usually worked for older girls and women (like their mothers), under their supervision and usually in their presence. They performed the traditional female tasks. They cared for babies and younger children, helped prepare food, carried in firewood and water, did other housework, helped gather wild foods, and did agricultural work. Boys might have done some things that were not preparation for traditional men's work. They might have run errands and done chores for their mothers. But usually, it seems, boys too were allowed to apprentice to work they would do as men. They played at hunting, or worked as herd boys, or farmed (depending on the case) with older boys and men. As they grew older, they were increasingly drawn into the man's work world.[5]

---

[3]William N. Stephens, *The Family in Cross-Cultural Perspective* (New York, Holt, Rinehart and Winston, 1963), p. 386.

William N. Stephens, "Children's Work in Traditional Societies and the Effect of Modernization," Meetings of the Society for Cross-Cultural Research, Boston University, 1974.

[4]Simmons, *Sun Chief*, pp. 25-72.

[5]Stephens, *Family in Cross-Cultural Perspective*, pp. 395-399.

The Dani of New Guinea, described by the anthropologist Karl Heider, exemplify a work-apprenticeship:

> [The Dani child] learns its own culture by informal observation. Children are allowed almost everywhere; they see and hear almost everything. They are never sent away, or told "this is adult business," or "it is time for bed." Children are often nuisances [but their parents let them watch].
>
> Among the Dani, there are no schools or no old men who spend the evenings telling the lore of the tribe to their grandchildren. The Dani child learns his way into his culture by *watching*, then *helping*, then taking a full part in activities. In all activities, battling, pig herding, gardening or rituals, Dani of various ages participate to various degrees.
>
> Children's *games* are an important means of learning and practicing adult activities. Nearly every major adult skill is previewed in a game. The numerous battle games . . . play gardens, play houses, compounds and watchtowers were made; play pigs are tended and butchered; girls carry around toy dolls and make toy skirts. Most play, even when it is unsupervised fun, in a real sense is educational.
>
> Children are given real responsibility at a young age. By the time they are five, they may take the family pigs out to the fields; before the girls are ten, they often have the care of babies for hours at a time. Children run errands and help with gardening and house construction, as soon as they are physically capable. Even though there is little overt coercion, by the time children are ten or twelve they are participating in most adult [work].[6]

This kind of apprenticeship needs primitive conditions. The work has to be physical work that children can see and comprehend. Chores must be sufficiently undemanding — of strength, experience, reliability, judgment, and delicacy of handling — so that children can do them. Really, a graded series of tasks has to be provided — increasingly more demanding and grownup — as the child advances through his apprenticeship.

Finally, children's help has to be needed. If a mother really needs her child's help, she will take the trouble to train the child early. (Otherwise, it is easier to simply do the work her-

---

[6]Karl Heider, *The Dani of West Irian*, Module 2 (Warner Modular Publications, 1972), p. 16.

self.) Needed work, as opposed to make-work, produces a different feeling in the child and in the parent. Needed work brings forth a different kind of educative process.[7]

This work-apprenticeship has been eroded by modern improvements. Life in many villages has been profoundly changed by labor saving devices: a water tap, installed at the village square; electrification; chances to earn cash and buy charcoal for fuel or to buy prepared food. These improvements strip away work opportunities for children. They have changed children's lives. There is some evidence that the children's character is changed as well.[8] Moving to the city does the same.[9]

What did this early work do for children? How was it character building? Anthropological studies do not permit a clear-cut, confident answer. (This needs no apology. Inquiries into the effects on character, of various things that happen in childhood, normally yield tentative answers.) The answers are in terms of trends and probable tendencies, not a clear-cut *does* or *does not*.

Evidence comes from village studies by John and Beatrice Whiting of Harvard. Helpfulness, responsibility, and nurturant, parental qualities appear to be some of the effects. This is hardly surprising. Helping out, children learn to be helpful. Given responsibility, they become responsible persons.

In the Whitings' villages, children were pressed into service at an early age. In the African case, over half the children were working by age four: carrying wood and water and helping with food preparation, gardening, housecleaning, and animal

---

[7]Beatrice B. Whiting and John W. M. Whiting, *Children of Six Cultures: A Psycho-Cultural Analysis* (Cambridge, Harvard University Press, 1975), pp. 70-110. The Whitings provide indirect evidence in support of these views.

[8]Nancy B. Graves and Theodore D. Graves, "The Cultural Context of Altruism: Development of Rivalry in a Cooperative Society" (Unpublished paper, South Pacific Research Institute, Auckland New Zealand), pp. 8, 38.

Whiting and Whiting, *Children of Six Cultures*, pp. 72-82.

[9]Graves and Graves, "Cultural Context of Altruism," p. 8.

Thomas S. Weisner, "The Child as Rural-Urban Commuter: Aspects of Socialization in City and Country Environments in Kenya" (Unpublished paper, Department of Anthropology, University of California at Los Angeles).

Beatrice B. Whiting, "The Effect of Urbanization on the Behavior of Children" (Unpublished paper, Cambridge, Harvard University).

care. In the Mexican and Philippine villages, the average age was closer to six; in the Okinawan and Indian, a little older still.[10]

The most primitive villages in their sample — with the fewest conveniences — had the most work for children. In these villages, mothers had to work harder. The Whitings think that these mothers were under particular pressure to train their children early to help out.[11]

The hardest-working children tended to score higher on the Whitings' measures of helpful-responsible-nurturant behavior. Also, some kinds of chores seemed to be more important than others. The life-giving work — caring for babies and helping to provide food — was most highly correlated with helpfulness, responsibility, and nurturance. Housecleaning was least correlated.[12]

The Whitings say:

> Carrying wood and water, the preparation and cooking of food, gathering, caring for animals, and caring for young siblings, particularly infants, are more likely to be performed by children of simpler cultures than by children of the more complex societies. It is our interpretation that the performance of these tasks provides one of the mechanisms by which children learn to be nurturant-responsible. All of these chores are intimately related to the daily life of the child aged 3 and 10 and must give him or her a feeling of personal worth and competence.
>
> The importance of chores related to the production and processing of food must be obvious even to a young child; if there is no wood or water the child suffers along with the other members of his or her family. The relation between gardening and eating, too, must be clear. Accompanying an

[10]Whiting and Whiting, *Children of Six Cultures*, p. 94.
[11]Ibid., p. 70-110.
[12]Ibid., pp. 84, 105-107.

Beatrice B. Whiting and John W. M. Whiting, "Task Assignment and Personality: A Consideration of the Effect of Herding on Boys" (Read before the Univeristy of East Africa Social Science Conference, Dar es Salaam, Tanzania, 1968).

John W. M. Whiting and Beatrice B. Whiting, "Altruistic and Egoistic Behavior in Six Cultures," in Laura Nader and Thomas Maretzki, eds.,*Cultural Illness and Health*, American Anthropological Association, Anthropological Studies no. 9 (61-64, 1973).

adult to the fields, picking maize, or digging potatoes and returning home, cooking, and eating them, is the daily experience of young children in these agricultural societies. Because adults are involved in these activities and it is clear that the mother is busy and needs help, the assignment of chores does not seem arbitrary and unnecessary. Participation must give the child a sense of worth and involvement in the needs of others.[13]

Working, children also seem to mature earlier. (The evidence is less good on this point.) The Whitings' findings could be interpreted in this way. Some anthropologists, observing working children, have commented on how grown-up they seemed.[14] I was struck by this when I studied a Spanish village. Even in Nova Scotia, I was impressed by the grown-up manner of some of the farm children.

Don Talayesva, after saying that learning to work was like play, describes how experienced and worldly-wise he soon became.

By the time I was six, therefore, I had learned to find my way about the mesa and to avoid graves, shrines, and harmful plants, to size up people, and to watch out for witches. . . . I slept out on the housetop in summer and sometimes in the kiva with the other boys in the winter. I could help plant and weed, went out herding with my father, and was a kiva trader. I owned a dog and a cat, a small bow made by my father, and a few good arrows. Sometimes I carried stolen matches tucked in the hem of my shirt collar. I could ride a tame burro, kill a kangaroo rat, and catch small birds, but I could not make fire with a drill and I was not a good runner like the other fellows. At the races people teased me and said that my feet turned out so far I pinched my anus as I ran. But I had made a name for myself by healing people. And I had almost stopped running after my mother for her milk.[15]

---

[13] Whiting and Whiting, *Children of Six Cultures*, pp. 103-106.
[14] Margaret Mead, *Coming of Age in Samoa* (New York, New American Library, 1949), pp. 24-29.
Beatrice B. Whiting, "Work and the Family" (Read before the International Conference of Women: Resource for a Changing World, Cambridge, Radcliffe College, 1972).
[15] Simmons, *Sun Chief*, p. 72.

These village children who were put to work seem not to have been troublesome in adolescence. In accounts of primitive villages, there is practically no mention of juvenile delinquency, or gangs, or rebelliousness, or oppositional teenage fashions. For modernizing villages, descriptions of this begin to appear. And of course it comes into full flower in our modern cities.[16] So, another possible effect of early work is: bypassed adolescent problems.

ROLE MODELING, IDENTIFICATION

Theories about role modeling go back to Freud. He called it *identification*. Some modern theorists speak instead of *modeling* or *imitation learning*. Working alongside the parent in an old-fashioned work-apprenticeship is the optimal condition for identification or role modeling. That is the way I interpret modern theorists on the subject.[17]

The ideal conditions were these:

• Adults' work and other activities were relatively easy for children to see and comprehend.

• Children could practice it in play.

• They could then actually put this in practice when they went to work.

• Much of the child's work tended to be in the role model's presence and under the role model's supervision.

A strong and successful identification can have various effects, depending on which theorist is read. Some of the imputed effects are:

• Wanting to be like the role model

---

[16]Stephens, "Children's Work."

[17]Albert Bandura, Dorothea Ross, and Sheila A. Ross, "A Comparative Test of the Status Envy, Social Power, and Secondary Reinforcement Theories of Identification Learning," *Journal of Abnormal and Social Psychology*, 67:527-534, 1963.

Carol R. Ember, "Feminine Task Assignment and the Social Behavior of Boys," *Ethos*, 1:424-439, 1973.

Eleanor E. Maccoby, "Role-taking in Childhood and Its Consequences for Social Learning, "*Child Development*, 30:239-252, 1959.

John W. M. Whiting, "Resource Mediation and Learning by Identification," in Ira Iscoe and Harold Stevenson, eds., *Personality Development in Children* (Austin, University of Texas Press, 1960), pp. 112-125.

• Copying the model's actions and beliefs
• A continuing desire to do the work (and other activities) that made up the role-modeling experience
• Feeling oneself allied with the model and similar to him

Other possible effects of identification are mentioned in literature.[18] Identification is viewed as a sort of psychological cement, tying children to their parents, the new generation to the old.

Remnants of the Work-Apprenticeship

If a modern parent *wanted* to give her child a peasant-style apprenticeship, she could not do it. The intimate village situation in which small children were first spectators on nearly all adult activities, played at doing adults' work, and then started apprenticing to it is gone, and it cannot be recreated.

Our own children — when they are little — are still eager to watch, imitate and "help." Few modern households can give children the unfolding series of tasks appropriate to their age. The closest approach to this is the training of some girls who apprentice in the home at being little mothers, doing housework, and caring for young children. Something resembling an old-fashioned apprenticeship is possible on some farms, and in certain other households where there is a lot of work to do. But most of us must let this opportunity go by. After our children

---

[18]Bandura, Ross, and Ross, "A Comparative Test,"

Ember, "Feminine Task Assignment,"

Alfred B. Heilbrun and Donald K. Frome, "Parental Identification of Late Adolescents and Level of Adjustment: The Importance of Parent-Model Attributes, Ordinal Position, and Sex of the Child, *"Journal of Genetic Psychology, 107*:49-59, 1965.

Dennis L. Krebs, "Altruism — An Examination of the Concept and a Review of the Literature, *"Psychological Bulletin, 73*:258-302, 1973.

Maccoby, "Role-taking in Childhood,"

Paul H. Mussen, "Some Antecedents and Consequents of Masculine Sex Typing in Adolescent Boys, *"Psychological Monographs, 75*:9, 1961.

Robert R. Sears, Lucy Rau, and Richard Alpert, *Identification and Child Rearing* (Stanford, California, Stanford University Press, 1965).

Darwin L. Thomas, Andrew J. Weigert, and Norma Winston, "Socialization and Identification with Parents: A Cross-National Study," Meetings of the American Sociological Association, New York, 1973.

Whiting, "Resource Mediation,"

pass the age when they are most eager to imitate our work and to help (age three to eight, more or less?) they may still have some desire to help out from time to time, but it is not the same.* Other habits have been learned in the intervening years. They are going to school, oriented to their peer groups, interested in having fun with their friends. They have other models to emulate.

To identify with means in part to *be under the influence of*, to *fall under the influence of*. In the modern situation, going to school and playing with friends rather than working alongside adults, the adult influence must be weaker. Children must be more peer oriented and less adult oriented.

— — — —

I went searching for remnants of the work-apprenticeship. I expected to find it on farms and in large families. This was partly correct. In some farms and large families children's work was still needed. But children started farm work, housework, and child care at a later age (than in the primitive villages), and their work was hedged by various restrictions.

Two other kinds of families also gave good work opportunities: (1) The latchkey child situation where the mother is absent, disabled, or works; an older daughter has to take her place, be in charge of the household, and mind the little ones. (2) Families with a working-on-projects life-style. The father is usually a fixer. The house is generally old, unmodernized, and needs a lot of maintenance. Most of these were in the country and not in the city.

If a home does not offer naturally occurring necessity conditions, in which the children cannot only be given work, but are *needed* to help out, then can any good substitute for this be arranged? The Whitings' answer would seem to be no. Some of my mothers disagree. What kinds of work can be found for these children, and what can be done to make up this deficiency — I searched for answers to these questions while doing my fieldwork.

---

*This is, of course, an empirical question that could be studied.

Chapter 3

CHILD CARE

Perhaps the most important thing that a child keeps practicing in the age period between three and six is being a
parent. It's clearest to see in a girl with her baby doll. First
come the simple actions — laying the doll in a bed, covering
it with a blanket, picking it up again, transferring it to the
doll carriage. As the months go by, the play becomes more
elaborate and realistic — giving bottles, changing diapers,
bathing, dressing and undressing, asking for an ever-more-
complete wardrobe. By four or five years of age a girl is
talking to her doll (or to a smaller child who has been assigned the role of baby) with the same words and tone of
voice that her mother uses in baby care. By keeping at it for
three years the child has mastered the essentials — not just the
manual skills but, more importantly, the attitudes — of
motherhood. After six, moving into a different stage of childhood, she can gradually put compulsive baby care aside until
she really needs to use it at twenty or twenty-five. And if you
had been able to make a tape recording of how she talked to
her doll at five, you'd be amazed at how closely it would
match her talk to her child twenty years later — much the
same proportion of affection, bossing, disapproval.[1]

WHEN a little girl has a younger child to care
for, her practice of the mother role becomes the real thing.
Some dramatic transformations can result. Margaret Mead, in
Coming of Age in Samoa, noted that the Samoans spoiled their
young children. But just when a child was developing into a
little tyrant, she was saddled with the care of a still younger
child. A metamorphosis occurred: from spoiled child to a responsible, rather harassed, child nurse. In this way, Mead said,
the rough edges were knocked off. By being put in a

---

[1]Benjamin Spock, *Problems of Parents* (New York, Fawcett World Library, 1962), pp.
118-119.

18

parental role, the child ceased to be babyish and selfish.[2] Or, as with the Kikuyu saying that the Whitings quote, " 'The youngest child is the spoiled child. . . . Since the youngest sibling has no younger brother or sister to care for, how can he learn to be responsible and nurturant? He will obviously end up selfish.' "[3]

Children in some large families show the results of this transformation. The older children are responsible and act like little parents. The youngest child is still "spoiled."

> The first time I visited Ursula's family, Ursie was six years old. Her sisters were Mary (eleven), Jenny (eight), Cynthia (three), and Cindy (two). The two youngest were called "the babies." Of the middle girls — Cynthia and Ursula — Cynthia (age three) was still babyish, demanding, and attention seeking. Ursula was a hardworking, responsible member of the team of adults and older children that cared for the babies and ran the household. Occasionally she regressed to babyish behavior, but this seldom happened.

Cynthia perhaps, by this time, has crossed the line from child role to mother role, like Ursula had previously done. Or perhaps, with less need for her help — only one remaining "baby," less housework, older children — the educative process in this family has changed, and she will not make the shift like her older sisters have done.

Ursula must have been following the example of her older sisters, as well as modeling after her parents. She had good examples to follow. This must be an important reason why she turned out so well.

> The Ryans live on a Nova Scotia farm and have nine children. There is a family tradition of parental nurturance. A beautiful family spirit evidently was established. Then it was passed along; the younger children were influenced by the older ones. Boys as well as girls, even the dog, seem nur-

[2]Margaret Mead, *Coming of Age in Samoa* (New York, New American Library, 1949), pp. 24-28.

[3]John W. M. Whiting and Beatrice B. Whiting, "Altruistic and Egoistic Behavior in Six Cultures," in Laura Nader and Thomas Maretzki, eds., *Cultural Illness and Health*, American Anthropological Association, Anthropological Studies no. 9 (1973), p. 60.

turant to the little ones, as well as hardworking, responsible, and sharing. The combined pressures of farm chores and child care may be especially conducive to this kind of behavior. This is true for all but the baby of the family, a four-year-old girl; she is "spoiled."

Maria was our *criada* in the Spanish village where we did fieldwork. She helped us care for our own baby. Her older daughters — Domiana, Juana, and Ysabel — visited us and helped too. All the girls were very maternal, hardworking, and good with the baby. Their little sister, Maria Jesus was four years old; she still acted like a baby herself. She sat on her mother's lap much of the time, sucked a pacifier, and exhibited spoiled-child behavior.

The Spanish people in this region make an enormous fuss over babies and little children. They exclaim over them (*/guapo niño!*) They want to touch them, to kiss them, to hold them. Little girls are extraordinarily maternal and, given a chance, play tirelessly with a baby. I wonder if Maria Jesus has now shifted over to responsible-maternal behavior; she is old enough, now, to be caring for babies herself. Perhaps, if she remains the youngest child, she will be a bit more "spoiled" than the others.

In this village, children vie for the privilege of being the baby-sitter. Girls, as they grow up, see this example around them. As soon as they can get their hands on a baby, they play the role for all it is worth. The example they follow is village-wide; it is "in the culture."

Child care is an important part of the work-apprenticeship in this village and in countless others. It can produce dramatic character changes, as Margaret Mead observed. The Whitings found empirical evidence for this. In their villages, the most responsible and nurturant children tended to be those who had done a lot of baby-sitting.[4]

In some primitive societies, boys and girls share the baby-sitting; however there is a tendency for girls to do most of it. And in some societies — like our own — girls do practically all

---

[4]Whiting and Whiting, "Altruistic and Egoistic Behavior," p. 61.

of it.[5] In my sample, few boys did child care. The boys' baby-sitting — what little there was of it — was the easiest, least demanding sort: They baby-sat older children. They rarely cared for infants and toddlers: Diapering and infant feeding was work for girls.

LEARNING TO BABY-SIT

When a little girl begins her child-care career, she has to be supervised. She performs limited duties under the mother's watchful eye. Then she goes on to greater responsibilities and less supervision, as she earns trust and gets older. Similarly, a career as a paid baby-sitter starts with "getting old enough," beginning work, and establishing a neighborhood reputation for trustworthiness.

Child care is very demanding. Patience, forebearance, caring, being able to play with the child with empathy and imagination — these and other desirable qualities come into play. However, *safety* considerations must be the main determinant of how much responsibility is given. Fear of accidents constrains the mother. In this respect, child care is like farm work and work with machines and the granting of autonomy and responsibility in other areas (such as driving, or traveling unsupervised). In the great differences between parents in safety standards and in views of "how old is old enough," it is also similar. The difference is: it is not the baby-sitter's safety which is feared for, but the baby's.

"How old is old enough" varies according to local custom. In a Nova Scotia sample I have polled, the proper age to begin baby-sitting ranged from nine to sixteen. The average age was twelve. The Whitings in their Six Culture Study also found

---

[5]Carol R. Ember, "Feminine Task Assignment and the Social Behavior of Boys," *Ethos*, *1*:424-439, 1973.

Sara B. Nerlove et al., "Natural Indicators of Cognitive Development: An Observational Study of Rural Guatemalan Children," *Ethos*, 2:265-295, 1974.

William N. Stephens, *The Family in Cross-Cultural Perspective* (New York, Holt, Rinehart and Winston, 1963), p. 367.

Whiting and Whiting, *Children of Six Cultures*, p. 149.

large differences, but the ages were much younger.[6] In their African villages, the average age to begin baby-sitting was seven; but it could be as young as five.[7]

The constraints on a mother, in giving her little one over to a baby-sitter, are these:

• The little child's age. The younger the child, the smaller the baby, the more vulnerable and needful; the more dangerous any lapses by the caretaker.

• The baby-sitter's age: Lapses are supposed to be more likely in younger children. For children working within the home under the supervision of their own mothers: trust can be earned for reliable child nursing duty, perhaps temporarily withdrawn when the girl backslides, re-earned . . . and as time goes by responsibility can increase. For baby-sitters working for strangers and near-strangers, there is probably a tendency for mere age to stand as an indicator of trustworthiness.

Lapses would include mistakes in judgment: not knowing what to do in an emergency, or making mistakes about what the little child can do and can't do. They would also include lapses of attention and care, as with an erratic child nurse who is attentive for awhile and then runs off to do something else.

A third constraint is realistic dangers in the environment — such as traffic — as well as accessibility of responsible adults.

A child nurse may work under supervision: The mother can be watching or be elsewhere in the house. Or, the mother or other responsible persons may be "around," as is often the case on the farm. In a village situation in which adults are responsible for each other's children and children normally play within view of someone, parents can relax their vigilance and children can wander more freely. This may be one reason why child nursing can commence so early in the Whitings' villages; a certain amount of supervision by the village is possible.[8]

In a typical child-care career, a little girl might start by doing a few things with a baby or toddler, under the mother's

---

[6]Whiting and Whiting, *Children of Six Cultures*, p. 95.
[7]Beatrice B. Whiting, "Folk Wisdom and Child Rearing," *Merrill-Palmer Quarterly of Behavior and Development, 20*:9-19, 1974.
[8]Whiting and Whiting, *Children of Six Cultures*, p. 98.

watchful eye; or she might entertain and play with an older and less vulnerable child — perhaps help keep him out of trouble — with a responsible adult being "around." As she gets older, she combines child care with more housework duties. Finally, she grows old enough (establishes sufficient trust) to be left in charge.

HELPING , SHARING, AND ALTRUISM

The Whitings correlated child care with a multidimensional scale. They called the scale *altruism-versus-egoism*.[9] Later, they referred to it as *helpful-responsible-nurturant*.[10]

Persons of this general type also occur in my sample. They are altruistic, or — to use other possible terms — they are helpful, sharing, giving, unselfish, "good sports," or "team players."[11] All but one of these altruistic persons are female — girls and young women. (The Whitings, too, found altruism correlated with femaleness.)[12] *All* of them had cared for younger children. Most were older sisters. They took care of younger brothers and sisters in fairly large families. This must be an especially good training ground for altruism. Unselfishness, willingness to step aside, to let other family members have their way, willingness to let others' needs take precedence over yours — the give-and take between brothers and sisters in a large family probably trains for this, especially so for the elder children, who are given child-care responsibility.[13]

They also did much of the housework and other kinds of work while they were minding the little ones. Their baby-sitting was not the easy, TV-watching type. They changed diapers, made up games for toddlers, cleaned up messes,

[9]Whiting and Whiting, "Altruistic and Egoistic Behavior," pp. 61-62. Other studies of altruism seem not to have looked at child care as a possible antecedent.
[10]Whiting and Whiting, *Children of Six Cultures*, p. 98.
[11]These are my impressions of their characters. I did not apply a measuring instrument, as the Whitings did.
[12]Whiting and Whiting, "Altruistic and Egoistic Behavior," p. 60.
[13]Children in large families tend to score high on altruism measurements. This literature is reviewed by Dennis L. Krebs, "Altruism — An Examination of the Concept of a Review in the Literature," *Psychological Bulletin, 73*:290, 1973.

washed and cooked, and took a large share of responsibility.

What predisposes toward being "altruistic" or "helpful-responsible-nurturant" seems to be: being a girl, doing baby-sitting, being an elder daughter in a fairly large family, and doing other work along with the baby-sitting. Another possible background factor — for which we have no evidence — is having a mother who is also this way. Following a good example must help.[14]

Virginia: The Team Player is Often Put-Upon

Virginia's mother returned to work when she was seven. For a while, the family had hired help. Sometime between the ages of ten and twelve, Virginia came into her age of responsibility. She remembers her routine as: make some of the breakfasts (there were two younger brothers, one younger sister), wash the breakfast dishes, and go off to school with the little ones; after school, come right home, supervise the kids, clean the house, and prepare dinner. After dinner, wash the dishes and begin on her homework.

Virginia thinks she did this work willingly. She can remember very little coercion. She wanted to have the house tidy and supper ready for her mother when she came home from work. But Virginia can remember feeling some resentment about housecleaning, since the sloppy family would have messed it up again within an hour. Her father was a bully. Her younger siblings were lazy, never helped with the work, and accused her of being bossy (evidently a frequent accusation toward older sisters).

Virginia's role in her family seems to have produced an incentive system something like the following. She felt sympathy for her hard-pressed mother. She felt she had to help. Being the responsible one must have been gratifying to her; and there was also external pressure — a slip-up in her duties risked her father's wrath. Also, if she didn't do it, the entire burden would

[14]John D. Krumboltz and Helen B. Krumboltz, *Changing Children's Behavior* (Englewood Cliffs, New Jersey, Prentice-Hall, 1972), p. 234. Krumboltz and Krumboltz also emphasize positive reinforcement; noticing and rewarding generous and unselfish acts.

fall on the mother. This is eventually what happened when Virginia left home to go to college. Her adult character? — strongly nurturant-responsible.

If I were to try to reconstruct how child care and other family work produces altruistic-helping-responsible character, it would be variations on this pattern. An original desire to help, and need for the child's help, is shaped into an incentive system and helping role, which keeps the child developing in the right direction.

Virginia is an example of a child who felt impelled to help, while her brothers and sister did not. It seems common in large families and farm families for the division of chores to be unequal and unfair: Some children develop into helpers, while certain of their brothers and sisters do not. Some families have a "spoiled baby." Other families are like Virginia's; several of the children are "lazy."

In a large family, older sisters are more apt to be the helpers (older brothers, too, in some cases.) Their parents need their help to manage the teeming household. Because of the pressure of necessity, the parents tend to put heavy demands on them. This evidently starts them developing in this way.

Bossard and Boll: The Martyrish Eldest Child

These researchers interviewed people who recalled their childhoods in large families — of six children or more. Bossard and Boll gathered more data than I did, and they discuss some features of large-family life that I would have missed. However, on several points, what they say sounds familiar:

• The typical large-family interaction style is: sharing, give-and-take, cooperative work; a minimum of individual attention; and more crises, but the crises are taken more calmly. (This last struck me as being particularly true of farm families.)

• Different children in the family develop specialized roles: the spoiled baby, the responsible eldest, perhaps a "mechanical" child, a "musical" child, a scapegoat child, and so on. (This again was most striking in my farm families.)

• One or several of the oldest children are very hardworking in the home; they act as lieutenants to the parents.

Bossard and Boll conclude that the eldest children tend to be "altruistic" to a fault:

> First, they tend to be put under pressure from an early age. From being put under pressure by others, they proceed to put themselves under pressure. Thus habits are formed which crystallize into patterns of responsibility. [p. 162]. . . . The oldest or an older one of the children in a large family develops marked habits of accountability, aiding the parents in their duties, sharing responsibilities, and taking over much of the rearing of the younger siblings. [p. 266]. . . . Patterns of sacrifice and service also manifest themselves early in life. Being the oldest means doing for others.[15]

The oldest child tended to sacrifice herself. She (or he) might quit high school, go to work, and help support the family. She might not go to college so that a younger brother or sister could go. She might delay getting married for similar reasons and pass up other opportunities.

The picture that emerges is of prematurely grown-up, rather martyrish eldest children, the product of excessive responsibility-pressure. The truism would seem to be: To produce a responsible child, you need merely put her in a situation in which she has to behave responsibly; however it can be overdone. (The father in one of my large families laments for his eldest daughter, "The poor child. She has the weight of the world on her shoulders.")

When the eldests marry, according to Bossard and Boll, they tend to choose weak, dependent mates, so they can go on being *the* responsible one in the family. They are apt to choose a widow(er) or divorcee who already has little children and who desperately needs help. On a marital happiness scale, the eldest did not score high, presumably because they tended to marry "losers."[16]

All this would not have occurred to me purely on the basis of my own case studies. I know a few people from large families who describe excessive workloads. Several can remember resenting too-great demands. As far as the self-sacrificing tenden-

---

[15]James H. S. Bossard and Eleanor S. Boll, *The Large Family System* (Philadelphia, University of Philadelphia Press, 1956), pp. 162-266.
[16]Ibid., pp. 266, 301.

cies are concerned, I had not noticed this for my large-family cases, possibly because my study method did not show it up. However, the people I think of as being especially altruistic, helping, and unselfish do seem to get themselves into situations in which they are exploited. This occurs mainly within the family: The spouse (or some other family member) takes advantage. I suspect one or two of them of seeking this role. But in the main, I think they are merely vulnerable to exploitation because of their helping natures, and are not drawn to it. Extreme responsiveness to the needs of others (one of the definitions of altruism) and sensitivity to moral constraints — this must be what keeps them working away in unfair family situations. This may also lead them to pass up some personal opportunities, in the fashion of Bossard and Boll's eldests. I know of instances of this for several of my altruistic cases. Nevertheless, it is my impression that these people do extremely well in life. They are loved and respected. I think it is a good way to be.

Summing Up Altruism

The altruistic people had child-care duty when they were young; most of them had a heavy workload of child care and housework. A mother who provides a good example is another possible background factor.

I suspect that the tendency to develop in this way is really fairly common among girls. At least it seems to be in the Nova Scotian sample. Its nexus appears to be maternal "instinct" or interest, which a good many of the girls showed stongly, early in life. If they got a good chance to practice this, cared for smaller children, and combined this with other housework and maternal duties, then quite possibly some of the associated "responsible" and "helpful" traits developed too. It looks like a need disposition that goes along with the traditional wife-mother role. (The ideal disposition, one might say.) Little girls grow into it, apprenticing to their mothers. At least, there is this tendency.

Another way of dealing with altruism is to break it down into its components. Four characteristics of the altruistic people are:

• They are hard workers within their homes. Hypothesis: children who are hardworking in their parents' homes grow up to be household workers in their own homes.

• They are givers and helpers, generous to family members and to friends and strangers. Hypothesis: This is encouraged by being required to help out in the home, in childhood.

• They are nurturant parents. (Put in the parental role, they relate to a little child in a giving, tender, diligent fashion.) Hypothesis: nurturant parents tend to get their start as baby-sitters, when they themselves were children and teenagers. Understudying a mother who provides a good example must help, too. (However I know a few parents — who seem very nurturant — who say they had absolutely no baby-sitting experience.)

• They tend to be good sports, undemanding, team players, willingly self-sacrificing in the family. This recalls Bossard and Boll's description of self-sacrificing elder siblings. I would guess that the large-family give-and-take is conducive to this: being responsible for younger siblings who preempt your attention, whose needs override your own, learning to stifle your resentment. Somehow, a nurturant-responsible disposition must come to take precedence over egoistic desires.

THE ADVANTAGES OF FAMILY HELPING

Later in the book we will meet other kinds of admirable young people. They also got their start helping out in the home. (There are a few exceptions.) Most of the managers and enterprisers were family helpers during childhood. The girls who learned to "cope by organizing" seem to have begun when they were children, helping their mothers. A good setting for a mechanical career is a home where the parents work on many household projects and involve the children in their work. Helping at home lays the foundation for various good lines of development.

I think that working at home tends to make children and teenagers easier to live with. Such children are less demanding, are more appreciative of things that are done for them, and are all-around nicer. This is merely my impression, and it is a biased impression at that. Perhaps, someday, someone will investigate this with systematic research.

"Marry a family-helper" seems like good advice. Minding the children; caring for a baby; doing housework; preparing meals; all sorts of cooperative projects, such as household repair and remodeling, gardening, and family camping trips; and the mere running of errands — all these should be easier if one spouse (or better yet, both) has the skills, the inclination, and the habits learned in childhood. (This too could be tested by systematic research.)

How can a mother give this training to her child, if she lives in a modernized, nonfarm home, and the child's help is not particularly needed?

Work in the home can be created. You can acquire a pet, start a garden, and do various other things. There is also housework of the clean-up-your-room variety. I know one mother who has kept her children busy this way.

Can artificial make-work substitute for the life-giving work of farm children and child nurses? The Whitings are rather discouraging on this point.[17] I think the average mother who tries to do this tends to slacken her demands after a while, feed the pet herself rather than continually nag the children, and do the children's chores. This is the course of least resistance. It takes an unusual mother to maintain the pressure on the children. This will be discussed in *Housework in Modernized Homes,* Chapter 7.

A teenage girl can eventually get a mother's helper job with another family. More limited baby-sitter jobs are available too. I am sure this can be good training, but I doubt if it takes the place of helping out within one's own home. For one thing, the girl is already so old. The period of early readiness has come and gone. This too is an open question: whether there is a critical period in childhood during which family helping must begin, in order to yield optimal results.

Parents who dare to be a bit unconventional can get around this by sending their children off for the summer — perhaps to stay with a relative — on a farm, or in a large family, where the children apprentice in a family work team.

---

[17]Whiting and Whiting, *Children of Six Cultures,* pp. 103-107.

I think that all children, boys as well as girls, should get baby-sitting experience. The benefits to the child are: practice at parenthood, and she (or he) gets to see what parenthood entails. There are also the possible character benefits. The educational value of child-care experience must depend on such factors as these:

• How old the child is when she starts
• Whether she cares for babies and toddlers as well as for older children
• How heavy her responsibilities, how total her immersion in the other home. (Mother's helper versus babysitter: see below.)

From the mothers' point of view: I think they need all the help they can get. Ours is one of the few societies in which a mother is taken out of circulation and isolated at home with her preschool children. Mothers have various ways of coping with this unnatural situation, but I think it tends to be bad for everyone. In the primitive villages, mothers continued with their lives outside the home, and child nurses and other adults helped them with their young children.[18]

Mothers are kept from making more use of baby-sitters by (for one thing) the notion that a baby-sitter must be fairly old — twelve or so — before she can be left unsupervised. This idea (which probably has much to be said for it, in some cases at least) combines with the babysitters' school schedules, the expense of paying the baby-sitter, the nine-to-five work day in possible jobs the mother might have, and the time consumed in driving back and forth. These are the constraints that keep the use of baby-sitters at its present level. This set of circumstances confines most mothers at home much of the time. I have no revolutionary proposal that would release them; only the suggestion that more and younger baby-sitters would be good for everybody: Even if a younger baby-sitter must be supervised, so that the mother cannot leave the house — this still seems to me to be a worthwhile arrangement.

---

[18]Stephens, *Family in Cross-Cultural Perspective,* pp. 366-368.

ARRANGING CHILD-CARE EXPERIENCES

These are the possible child-care arrangements outside one's own home:

1. *Babysitting:* A teenager is paid seventy-five cents per hour (or whatever) for minding the neighbors' kids. When the baby-sitter comes, the parents normally leave the home. The baby-sitter may play with the children, perhaps change a diaper, give a bottle, prepare a simple meal; or, she may do little more than watch television. Two possible shortcomings that babysitting may have is: being paid changes the spirit of the relationship, so any benefits are reduced; a more serious charge, I think, is that most baby-sitting jobs are too limited to be of much significance as training. However, there are all kinds of baby-sitting, ranging up to the mother's helper who lives in for the summer and does everything.

Even limited baby-sitting jobs have more to them than meets the eye. Baby-sitter instruction booklets, such as those produced by the Canada Safety Council, give long checklists of things to remember, prepare for, and look out for. The babysitter's essential function is to play the role of responsible adult: deciding issues that come up, saying no or yes and coping with emergencies, large and small. A single evening of baby-sitting might offer little or nothing in the way of new learning or challenge. However, an entire baby-sitting career, spanning jobs in numerous homes over a period of several years, should present many situations that require coping and responsible deciding.

2. *Mother's Helper:* This is an all-around household worker and mother's lieutenant in a home where there is much work to do. In my files are two types of mother's helper jobs. One is a live-in arrangement — a summer job on Annapolis Valley farm, or staying with relatives in Ontario, or traveling with a family that is on vacation. In the other kind of mother's helper job, the girl continues to live at home; she goes to her job after school and on weekends. I have several descriptions of such arrangements which sound like profound learning experiences for the girls. They were hired because the mother was

working, was disabled, or for some reason really needed help. They stayed with the family over a number of years, helped bring up the children, became "one of the family," and were themselves changed. For example Anne, described in the *Failed Modeling* chapter, changed from a lazy nonhelper (her role in her own family) to a hardworking little mother.

3. *Helping out a relative:* perhaps on a farm, or in a large family, or helping an aunt who has a new baby. Some older children without younger siblings to care for do have the opportunity to get this experience in a relative's home. It can take the form of summer visits or (if the other home is in the same town) a long-term, after-school and weekends arrangement.

There is one very admirable boy in the sample who cared for his grandmother (Irv, mentioned in the *Managing Affairs* Chapter), and a girl who cared for a number of aged relatives. In both cases this was live-in duty, with similarities to child care.

4. This raises the possibility that *other kinds of caretaking*, not just child care, may give similar training and benefits. There is also volunteer work with the aged, with the handicapped, or with children: in nursing homes, hospitals and other institutions, and home visits. When a teenager is old enough there are paid jobs available in hospitals, not to mention in organized programs for children — camp counselor or summer playground worker.

Some girls who started with child care at home went on to do several of these other jobs. These give breadth to a caretaking career. Ideally, I think they are a supplement to child care, rather than a substitute.

Finally, parents can give their child a dog or a cat. One argument for pets is that they give children quasi-parental training. Perhaps there are cases in which there is some truth to this, and perhaps not.

5. Some teenagers work in *day-care centers*. [19] This can be part of a child development course that the teenager is taking in high school. In the best possible arrangement, such as that described for the Princeton, New Jersey, high school program,

---

[19]Whiting, "Folk Wisdom," p. 18.

the young apprentice gets high quality on-the-job teaching. Thus she might learn much more, become more aware and more sensitized, than she would by merely working on her own as a baby-sitter.[20] This sounds like another supplement to child-care experience within the home, but it does not sound like a substitute for it.

6. Finally, the right kind of *neighborhood play group* may help make up for the lack of younger brothers and sisters to care for. I have in mind mixed-age play groups of the sort that I have seen in several rural hamlets. Of course parents have little control over whom their children play with, once they have decided where they will live. Although I have heard descriptions of mixed-age play groups for two city neighborhoods, I think this is more common in the country.

In some play groups, all the children are about the same age. Certain kinds of play tend to encourage age-segregation. Competitive sports, played by boys, are especially apt to be this way, I think. In other play groups, the older children are more tolerant of the little ones who tag along and are more generous about including them in their games. Another dimension that divides play groups is the imaginative quality of the play. When the two characteristics are combined, as a result of an imaginative leader or leaders, the group may have a rich assortment of games and make-believe play that can simultaneously interest the older kids and include the younger ones.

A child so fortunate as to live in such a neighborhood gets training in relating to younger children in a quasi-parental fashion. The example of the older children, and the rules of the game as they have been defined, can influence behavior along these lines. No doubt this is more characteristic of girls' play than of boys'. Competitive sports is its enemy. However, if the spirit is strong enough, it can transform the activity. Visiting farms in Nova Scotia, I have played in baseball games that had players of both sexes and all ages (down to age four), in which no one kept score, which were a hilarious spoof on baseball.

Why should this be more likely in small communities? The psychologist Roger Barker has written the definitive analysis,

---

[20]Suzanne S. Fremon, "Parenthood Training for Teenagers," *Parents Magazine*, 44-45, 1975.

based on his fieldwork in Oskaloosa, Kansas. In a small community there is never enough competent personnel — for a baseball game, or the high school play, or the town band, or for offices in civic organizations. So people learn to put up with a few incompetent actors in the play, musicians in the band, players in the game, and so on. Not only is tolerance learned; this squelches any deadly serious tendencies, such as I remember from my own midwestern upbringing, playing baseball, basketball, and football.[21] A baseball game with Lucy at shortstop and Snoopy in centerfield is hardly meaningful as competition between two teams. The point of the game has to be found elsewhere. Accommodations have to be made. For children, this means there is encouragement to play less competitively, to include the little ones, and to do so with forebearance.

I found this style of play in rural neighborhoods. Rural upbringing has its advantages. This is one of them. Other advantages are exposure to farm work, and learning various self-maintenance skills. Later some of the big city's resources, which facilitate the careers of teenage hobbyists, managers, and enterprisers, will be described. First, however, let us pursue the advantages of rural life.

---

[21]Roger Barker and Herbert Wright, *Midwest and Its Children* (New York, Row, Peterson, 1954).

Chapter 4

FARM WORK

Lorraine lives on a beautiful farm with apple orchards and cows, and a sweeping view over the Annapolis Valley in Nova Scotia. Her mother is a gracious woman who has raised five children, while doing a farmwife's work. The house is large and spacious, but it is short on comforts and conveniences. Often the house is cold. As you may know, a farmwife not only has constant toil and many little hardships and inconveniences; but usually there is an emergency, something special to cope with: a cow is giving birth; or there is a disease in the chicken house; the water pipes are frozen; it is preserving time for strawberries; company is coming; or the baby is vomiting. Crisis is normal.

Lorraine's mother goes through the day, does her work, tends her wood stove, takes care of her family, and serenely handles the emergencies that come her way. Lorraine (age twelve) is her lieutenant. She minds the little children. She helps out in the kitchen. She goes down the road to her grandmother's and mows the lawn for her, and does other work after school. She joins in, such family activities as berry picking.

Lorraine seems nurturant toward the little ones, responsible, helpful, a good sport. The hardships and work on the farm — she is used to it; she does not seem to mind. Lorraine appears to be copying after her mother.

I WENT to live on farms, thinking they would come closet to the work-apprenticeship conditions of the primitive villages. Some people did not encourage me in this view. A midwestern 4-H leader told me, "Most farm kids hardly do chores any more. Their lives are pretty much like city kids'." This depends — I later found out — on how modernized the farm is. I have seen (and heard described) many different kinds of farms and different sorts of rural living

35

arrangements. Modern laborsavers do eliminate a lot of children's work. School also takes children away from farm work. Dangerous machinery limits what they can do. Still, many farms do offer a work-apprenticeship. It bears some resemblance to the primitive villages.

How do farm children turn out? It is my impression that they tend to be helpful and responsible; and there is early maturity of a sort. Can city kids find farm work and benefit from it? Yes, if certain obstacles are overcome.

FARM CHILDREN'S APPRENTICESHIPS

One thing that farm life seems to do is to *really* engage the interest of children. The farm animals, the machinery, the rich assortment of farm activities to watch — the children are fascinated. They want to watch, to tag along, and if possible to help. This is most safely said of little children in the stage of life when they want to "help" but cannot be loaded with too much drudgery. Older children who know, firsthand, the arduous nature of farm work may have different ideas. However I think some powerful incentives can grow up around farm work, involving the sense of grown-up competence and mastery, and being a needed member of the family work-team.

So the first step in the village-style learning-to-work process — children eagerly watching adults' work, imitating it, and wanting to help — this step must be taken by children who live on farms. (City children who visit the farm must likewise have their interest aroused.)

When we come to the second step of the learning-to-work process — gradually being drawn into the family work team and helping in small ways — here there are more difficulties. The most fascinating things the farmer does — with machinery and with the animals — also tend to be the most dangerous. The very activities that farm boys emulate so as to play at them — they must be kept at a distance from these, for safety's sake. Therefore, farm boys are held back from participating in some of the more interesting work, usually until sometime in their teens. How long, and how much of the work, depends on the type of farm operation, and the machinery used, and the parents' safety standards — which vary widely. A boy is introduced piecemeal to barn work and work with machinery, under fairly close supervision, and observing numerous taboos. This must have been somewhat true even in simpler days. Men and older boys did the team driving, the axe wielding, the shooting and so on while little boys — not old enough yet — watched from a distance. But the tractors, combines, bailers, mowing and threshing machines, and other mechanical devices must exclude farm boys from even more work now, and exclude them until a later age.

Farm girls can apprentice to their mothers, less constrained by safety precautions. As with nonfarm families, girls' role modeling is less interfered with by modern work conditions.[1]

Household laborsavers, as well as farm machinery, limit children's work. On farms as elsewhere, these have eliminated a lot of the simple, fetch-and-carry, low-skill, low-strength, low-responsibility tasks that children have done in the past. In my sample, I have rural families who lack various modern conveniences. The omission of one of these provides work for children: carrying water from an outside well; helping with some of the housework that is created by lack of hot-and-cold running water; emptying a bucket that serves as an indoor toilet; and, especially, cutting and carrying wood for the wood stove. In Nova Scotia the wood stove represents a life-style. The farmwife arranges her day in terms of the stove's requirements. A child in a woodstove family knows his work is basic and necessary. "When the woodbox is empty the house gets cold."

One could make a scale to represent how modernized a house is. In addition to the type of stove, there are other possible modern improvements: electrification, running water, hot water, adequate hot running water (in some rural homes it is unreliable or meager), a furnace, the adequacy of furnace heating, laborsavers in the kitchen . . . and on up the scale to pure comforts and frills such as carpeting. I am sure that how hard children work, doing chores, has much to do with

---

[1]Talcott Parsons, *Essays in Sociological Theory: Pure and Applied* (New York, Free Press of Glencoe, 1949), p. 257.

how modernized the house is.

Another trend in farming, which is directly related to machines and modernization, is the shift from diversified small farms to capital-intensive, specialized, large-scale cash cropping.[2] My Uncle Bill's farm had laying hens, milk cows, a milk separator on the back porch that provided, as a by-product, skim milk used for slopping the hogs; bee hives set in a fruit orchard; nut trees; a smokehouse; a truck garden; and small fields planted in crops. This kind of small, diversified operation, with a minimum of business with the outside and a lot of self-support, is the typical postfrontier farm traditional to North America. Except for its isolation, it was not so different from the village families described by the anthropologists. In poor, backward areas this kind of life-style continues today — usually with fewer farming activities and often combined with sporadic employment in town or with welfare, unemployment, or pension checks. But the farmers who have kept up and really remained in business, as farmers, are now more specialized. With them, there are either no chickens to tend at all, or there are 14,000 in an automated, two-story hen house. Either there are no cows to milk, or there is a herd of thirty to be run through a milking parlor twice a day. "Crops" may be nonexistent, or the one or two crops may stretch almost to the horizon and be cultivated by thundering machines. This means fewer jobs that children can do.

There is one more way in which farm upbringing diverges from a traditional work-apprenticeship. Most farm youth will never take over the farm and become farmers themselves.[3] The years of doing chores, of graduating to progressively more mature tasks, of learning how to farm from their parents, is prob-

---

[2]William E. Amos, "Child Labor Standards and School Attendance as Related to Rural Youth," in Lee G. Burchinal, ed., *Rural Youth in Crisis: Facts, Myths, and Social Change* (Washington, D.C., Office of Juvenile Delinquency and Youth Development, Department of Health, Education and Welfare, n.d.), p. 336.

[3]Amos, "Child Labor Standards," p. 336.

James H. Copp, "Family Backgrounds of Rural Youth," in Lee G. Burchinal, ed., *Rural Youth in Crisis: Facts, Myths, and Social Change* (Washington, D.C., Office of Juvenile Delinquency and Youth Development, Department of Health, Education and Welfare, n.d.), p. 41.

ably not a preparation for their lifework. Some youths cannot wait to leave the farm for easier nonfarm occupations. Others want to stay; some of them will stay on, but their futures are uncertain. This uncertainty must cast its shadow before it. Not automatically assuming that you will do what your father does — as with the prototypical peasant boy, learning from his father — must tend to undermine, to some extent, any role-modeling process.

Keeping these qualifications in mind, in Nova Scotia, the nearest approach to the old work-apprenticeship seems to be offered by subsistence farms (throwbacks to my Uncle Bill's) and by dairy farms that are not too mechanized (and which probably are not economically viable in the long run). Other operations — chicken farms, apple orchards, cranberries, pigs, beef cattle, sizeable field crops — seem to offer less work for children. There are certain exceptions to this, as we shall see.

CHARACTERIZING FARM WORK

As you may know if you have ever lived on a farm, farmers work so much harder than city people do that there is simply no comparison. Farm youth who grow up and leave the farm, for the university or for jobs in the city, say that any work they do thereafter seems soft and undemanding. My characterization of farm work would be, first of all:

1. *Much* work: completely off the work scale that applies to city folk. (This is true for bona fide working farms. There are people who live in the country but do not support themselves by farming; these would be exceptions. In addition, farm families have certain members who do not do their share.)

2. Hardship: waking to a cold house, going out into the barn in the January predawn . . . cold, wet, dirt and mess; rough, harsh conditions, arduous and physically taxing.

3. Some monotony; milking, for example, is something like working on a factory production line. But the day-in day-out farm tasks add up to diversity: it is not the stereotyped work of a factory hand.

4. The work begins and ends with the machine: the chain

saw, the tractor and its attachments, the milking equipment, the sprayers. Machines have to be cared for, cleaned, lubricated, and fixed when they won't work. When a farmer starts a job he gets out the machine, tries to start it, and often has to tinker with it. Someone on the farm must be a mechanic. Boys who show mechanical talent must get enormous encouragement and recognition. Even rural people who are not farmers seem to spend a lot of time tinkering; they fix things and make things around their homes, and do for themselves.

5. The farmwife and her farm-girl lieutenant manage diverse projects, some revolving around the house, kitchen, and wood stove, and others taking them outside. Normally there is a crisis, as in the case of Lorraine and her mother. There is usually mess and disorder. The farmwife's style is casual; brisk perhaps, in hectic periods, but casual. I think farmwives are better equipped, than city mothers, to care for babies and very young children. Hardened as they are to confusion and mess in the house, and to hard work; with their casual household style; with a higher likelihood(?) of having other people in the home to share the burden — a new child represents one more project to be worked into the operation they manage, to be blended in with other duties. They also have other advantages, as compared with city mothers. Motherhood does not "take them out of circulation." A new child should have plenty to stimulate and interest him.

6. Many chores are done by family work teams. The emergencies and special projects call forth spontaneous teamwork. The work style I have observed on farms emphasizes "pitching in" and "helping out."

This completes my characterization of farm work, which is of course overgeneralized; which perhaps — who knows? — is somewhat positively slanted.

Although the dangerous machinery keeps children away from some of the farmer's work, there is still so much happening in and around the house, so much nonmechanized work (berry picking, canning, gardening, and so on), and so much fixing to observe, that a child can be involved in farm work continuously, as a spectator and helper. He sees a lot of pitching in and helping out. He must get drawn into this.

The dangerous machines put limits on where a small child can go and what he can do; but in other ways the child is encouraged to join in. On the farms I observed, people were tolerant of little helpers who made a mess. This certainly makes it easier to work small children into various activities. For example the vegetable garden would be large and cultivated by a tractor. It would not be meticulously kept. Parents could allow a toddler to "help" in the garden; if he damaged some plants, that was all right.

To sum up what there is on the farm to motivate children to work:

• Their interest is aroused by the animals, the machinery, and the rich variety of things to do and see; they have models to emulate; and they are drawn into work projects.

• There is the pressure of necessity. (This varies, of course.) At least some of the work is basic and life-giving. ("When the woodbox is empty the house gets cold.") Parents may teach little children how chores make food. ("My mother took me into the garden. She pulled up baby carrots. She told me, 'These are going to grow and get big!' ")

• Finally there is the we-working-together family spirit. It comes out in talk around the dinner table. Farm families speak of money-making schemes they have tried in the past and new schemes they might try. They discuss work problems: bad weather, crop infestations, machine breakdowns. They are operators of a business enterprise. Together as a family, they have a history of joint ventures, hopes and plans, emergencies coped with, travail and disappointment. (Most of the farms I visited were, as businesses, doing badly.) Conflict and recriminations are evident, but so is this we-working-together spirit.

HOW FARM CHILDREN TURN OUT

We should have a this-culture replication of the Whitings' work, comparing farm children with nonfarm children, scoring them on measures of helpfulness, responsibility, and altruism and correlating this with the work they do. (Other family types could also be compared: large family versus small family, modernized house versus unmodernized.) My impression is that I have seen much helpful, sharing, parental, and responsible behavior by children and adolescents on farms. The cross-cultural studies (*see* Chap. 2) do show that when a rural-urban comparison is made, the rural children are higher on altruism measures. The same is true for children in traditional societies and "backward" areas, as compared with children in western societies.[4]

How about early maturity and bypassed adolescent problems? Farm children when they are working at home do seem surprisingly grown-up. However, I have heard it said that certain rural children seem "immature" at school or in an urban setting, in the sense of acting awkward and shy, backward, and retarded in their ability to deal with the outside world.

In regard to adolescent problems, the psychological literature reporting rural-urban comparisons finds country youth sometimes better, sometimes worse, and sometimes about the same as city youth. In general, rural teenagers do not score particularly well on questionnaire-based indicators of adjustment or family relations, teacher ratings of responsibility, or on the MMPI or other personality tests.[5]

These findings can be discounted. The comparisons are generally *rural* versus urban, not farm versus nonfarm, and only one-fourth of rural people live on farms.[6] Effects of isolation, poverty, and other things associated with rural life are mixed with any effects of farm work. Whatever the reason, the benefits

------

[4]Nancy B. Graves and Theodore D. Graves, "The Cultural Context of Altruism: Development of Rivalry in a Cooperative Society" (Unpublished paper, South Pacific Research Institute, Auckland, New Zealand), pp. 8, 38.

[5]Lee G. Burchinal, "The Rural Family of the Future," in James H. Copp, ed., *Our Changing Rural Society* (Ames, Iowa State University Press, 1964), pp. 180-183.

Robert C. Bealer, Fern K. Willits, and Peter R. Maida, "Myth of a Rebellious Adolescent Subculture: Its Detrimental Effects for Understanding Rural Youth," in Burchinal, *Rural Youth in Crisis*, pp. 49-50.

Dale B. Harris, Kenneth E. Clark, Arnold M. Rose, and Francis Valasek, "The Measurement of Responsibility in Children," *Child Development*, 25:28, 1954.

Starke R. Hathaway, Elio Monachesi, and Lawrence A. Young, "Rural-Urban Adolescent Personality," *Rural Sociology*, 24:331-346, 1959.

[6]Copp, "Family Backgrounds of Rural Youth," p. 35.

of a farm upbringing do not come through on these question-
naires. But even if it were true that farm youth were not particularly advantaged, all told, city youth might still benefit from
farm experiences.)

Some farm children are keen workers and seem to be emulating a parent. This is the most readily observable behavior
that might be the result of role modeling. But other youth are
grudging workers. They are "lazy"; or they have no aptitude or
interest for some or for practically all of the work; or they are
hardworking enough, but they look forward to the time when
they can leave. Some farmers must mishandle their children's
apprenticeship so that any modeling fails; the child is "turned
off" rather than "turned on." This is discussed in the *Failed
Modeling* chapter.

In some of my families the division of chores seems glaringly
unfair. One child is hardworking, while a brother or sister may
do very little. The work-training process yields different results
within the same family, and the children slip into their respec-
tive roles: the son who is "mechanical"; another son who is
"bookish" instead; the "steady worker"; the "spoiled baby of
the family"; and so on. In other families, everyone seems to be
working fairly hard. Finally, I found a few successful farms
with modernized houses, in which the kids were watching television in their pajamas. Having been released from necessity
pressure, the parents evidently let up on their work demands.
The result appeared to be: city-type teenagers.

WHY FARM EXPERIENCE SHOULD
BE GOOD FOR CITY YOUTH

Whatever the merits of farm upbringing for role modeling
and for teaching responsibility and helpfulness, it may be that
this only works for children who are in the family; it may not
work for visitors. On the other hand, it is possible that some of
this influence can "rub off" on a visiting youth, under optimal
conditions and sufficiently long exposure. I have seen one particular case of a farm apprenticeship where this seems to have
happened. I have heard about a number of other cases in which

it appears something of this sort occurred.

But the strongest and simplest arguments in favor of farm work — in my opinion — have to do with hardening, work habits, and mechanical skills. Conditioning to some of the hardships one encounters on farms, and to the very high and arduous work standards, should prepare a youth to cope with, and be comfortable in, a wider range of situations in later life. The same is true for any mechanical training and other self-maintenance skills he picks up. I am thinking of such future situations as camping out; living in other primitive conditions; being able to maintain a country home or an old house; or adventuring and living in underdeveloped countries. (The example I have in mind, from personal experience, is the way one lives while doing anthropological fieldwork.) Many of us have been sheltered from realities of these sorts. Now it seems prudent that youth be better prepared, than we were, to take care of themselves.

FARM WORK OPPORTUNITIES

The idea that farm life would be good for nonfarm kids is an old one. But attempts to do anything about it run into difficulties. In Canada for example, there have been efforts by the government to send youth out to the farms; but the benefits to youth seem rather modest, in proportion to the time and dollars spent on programs.*

---

*Under an apprenticeship program, a dairy farmer, for example, after having demonstrated that he cannot get the hired help he needs, can take on an apprentice. The apprentice is paid through a Canada Manpower Industrial Training Grant. I have heard of a similar program in the United States. A youth can apprentice as a farm machinery operator under a farmer's supervision. After an apprenticeship period, if the farmer certifies that he is competent, the youth becomes a full-fledged operator.

Other programs have sent teenagers to live on the farm for brief periods:

● Ontario's Junior Agriculturalist Program gives a summer-long farm experience to two hundred high school students. It is for youth with no previous farm experience, who say they are planning an agriculture-related career.

● A similar program in Alberta (perhaps discontinued by now).

● A rural-urban exchange program in Ontario (now discontinued); younger adolescents were given a week's exposure to farm living.

These exposure-type programs show a concern over the problem, but they seem ➡

I questioned people who ran government programs, as well as the farmers themselves, county agents, and rural sociologists, in an effort to understand what the problem was.

Which farmers need outside help that teenage farm hands might provide? The answer seems to be practically everyone.

How are visiting teenagers used now? In general, the answer is they are used primarily like other migrant laborers are used; in work gangs. This supplies only a part of the help a farmer needs. There remains an unmet need for all-purpose farm hands. Also, in terms of the youth's own benefit from the work, a work gang offers a minimal farm experience. The obvious next question is:

Why do farmers not take on more city youths, as true apprentice farmhands?

There is also the question, how do city youths find farm jobs? And there is the manpower question: How to do a better job of supplying youthful farm hands to farmers who need workers? Research needs to be done on this manpower question. I heard expert opinions on this subject, but I could not find any relevant research.

The experts agreed that small, mixed farms and subsistence farms still offer much work for the children of the family, especially when the father commutes to a job and someone must stay home and take care of things. (Of course these farms would be the least able to pay a farmhand; however they could take in a relative or a young person who was working for the

---

rather insignificant to me. First of all, small numbers of youth are served. (There are administrative constraints on the programs' size, having to do with their temporary summertime nature, difficulty in getting farm placements, and fear of bad publicity from "bad" cases.) In addition, they offer exposures rather than continuous training. They are not apprenticeships. The youth is not working on the farm long enough to really learn new and useful skills or to have his character molded. That is my opinion, at any rate. Rather, to use a ministry official's phase, "It is to show them what farm life is like." I would rank it with other exchange programs (living with another family) as an educational experience, probably more beneficial than school trips and summer camps, but less worthwhile than bona fide farm training.

What the government can do more efficiently is play the role of employment agency. Canada Manpower sets up summer offices to hire large numbers of fruit pickers, tobacco pickers, and other harvest hands. State Employment offices in the United States play a similar role. The limitation here is that youth who take such jobs usually work in work gangs; their exposure to farm life is quite limited.

experience.) Several people spoke on the subject of how large-scale mechanization delays the age at which boys can do much work and how it eliminates farm-hand employment for youths (except for work gang and harvest hand jobs).

The following three types of farms were mentioned as sometimes, in certain cases, offering work for children. (In other cases the work would be too grown-up.)

• Irrigation farming in the West: On some of these farms, children can help with such tasks as opening and closing irrigation gates.

• Cattle ranches: For jobs such as checking the fences; raising animals generally.

• Orchards: Even if growers use migrant labor, it is just for picking. There are many other jobs — especially spraying — that have to be done by people who are there all the time.

One sociologist, Professor Harry Dillingham at the University of Cincinnati, maintains that *all* farms are chronically short of labor and could use more help. At peak times especially — harvest, the growing season, the breeding season — the need is especially acute. Outside of a period of winter doldrums, the farms could use more workers.

Several constraints account for the gap between *need* and actual *use*. The easiest way to use hired help is on work gangs, doing routinized short-term jobs: harvest hands, pickers, corn detasselers; helping with the haying; and so on. When one sees or hears about nonfarm youth doing farm work, it is generally labor gang work of this sort. From the boy's point of view, the pay is relatively good, and these jobs are probably the most accessible and the best advertised. Beyond this the benefits must be minimal: a brief hardening experience, a view of another way of life. For teenagers, all grueling slave labor must have a certain challenge value. If the youth can endure and handle the job, then he must feel more a man, feel better about himself. No doubt this can be a real reward, but it can be supplied by many other kinds of production jobs.

From the farmer's point of view, a work gang, segregated off in some part of his farm doing a repetitive job like picking, is easy to supervise. Whatever teaching that has to be done is easy and brief. His time investment and risk is minimal. Work gangs seem to be viable from a manpower point of view. However they take care of only a portion of the help that the farmer needs. He also needs a "hired man" (or hired men or youths) who works with him continuously and helps out in the myriad jobs and emergencies that he must cope with day by day. Farmers who do not have working-age sons have been known to go out of business for want of a hired man. I know two farmers who have taken into their homes bizarre mental patients, so desperate is their need for a farmhand.

There are a number of readily observable reasons (and perhaps more undiscovered reasons) why farmers have trouble finding this kind of help. Many farmers could not afford a fully competent adult. A boy? Here the main problem is the farmer's investment of teaching time. Teaching his own son, the farmer spends years. A long apprenticeship is involved in building up the work habits, skills, and knowledge of a semi-autonomous farm worker. If the farmer took on an untrained boy, he would first of all have to spend a long period of teaching and close supervision. Immediately, he faces a dilemma that is common to apprenticeships to complex and varied occupations: The apprentice does useful work to the extent that he can be put on repetitive, simple jobs and left unsupervised. When the farmer spends time teaching him to do new things, then the farmer must spend time with him; the farmer is investing his own time and taking the apprentice away from productive work. In other words, when the apprentice is learning he is not producing very much; when he is producing he is not learning. In such a situation, the supervisor (in whatever line of work) is tempted to stint on the apprenticeship and keep the youth on simple, productive jobs.[7]

The farmer will try to teach his own son; but with outsiders, the temptation must be strong to limit the boy's scope. This is often a rational way of handling this dilemma. If the boy is not an apt pupil, or if the farmer is not a good teacher, the return on the investment may not be good. If the boy quits before he has returned the investment of time, then the farmer has lost

---

[7]Howard S. Becker, "School is a Lousy Place to Learn Anything In," in Blanche Geer, ed., "Learning to Work," *American Behavioral Scientist, 16:* 1972.

out. If the apprenticeship is a brilliant success, the boy will probably quit anyway when he finishes high school, in order to make his career elsewhere. I have observed one particularly admirable case of a successful farm apprenticeship of this sort, in which the boy must have benefited greatly by modeling himself after the farmer; and that is how it ended.

For some farmers the teaching role is congenial. If they get an apt and eager boy, they are willing to do it. Also, various compromises can be made — teaching the boy some skills and not teaching him others — to make it a less risky investment for the farmer. This seems to be the most worthwhile summer farm experience a youth could hope for: living with a farmer who was a good teacher, who was willing to give him a limited apprenticeship.

Farmers who do not wish to take on raw recruits can try to find hired hands who already have some background and who need less teaching and supervision. This is a good reason for hiring country youths. Even country lads who do not live on farms probably have better preparation than do city boys. They have probably watched and participated in the sort of mechanical fixing that is integral to farm work. They are likely to be more prepared for the chores and the all-around life-style. My impression is that farmers do prefer country boys over city boys. Also, country lads are more apt to hear of farm jobs and be recommended through friends and relatives. Still, it seems hard for operators of family farms to pay competitive wages. If the farmer gets a reasonably competent boy, or man, he is apt to lose him soon. This leaves the door open again, for relatively untrained youth from the city to come out and apprentice, summers and weekends. This leads us, too, to some of the other difficulties with taking city boys onto the farm.

Supervising an apprentice must be temperamentally exacting. Some farmers are not good at it. Their sons tend to leave home, and they have troubled relationships, thereafter, with hired help. There are filling station operators and other small business men, who need to hire youth, who have the same problem. But the farmer's situation is more difficult than the gas station's operator's because so much teaching and supervision is required.

There are other problems. Since farms tend to be isolated, it may be difficult for the hired hand to get home at night. He may have to live on the farm. As far as the boy's experience is concerned, this is fine and part of the benefits. But it is a constraint on some farmers hiring help.

Then there is the dangerous farm machinery. The farmer's children have been trained to observe the safety precautions. Visiting children are harder to control. It can be dangerous even to let them *play* unattended, let alone work. Several informants stated there was more scope for visiting girls from the city than for boys. Especially if they have had previous mother's helper experience, they would have more transferable skills, and they would be less in the way of the machines.

A number of farmers, who needed hired help and did not have any, voiced the pessimistic opinion that few nonfarm youths would want to work on the farm: The work would be too hard; there would be too much hardship and not enough excitement; the pay would be too low. No doubt there is some truth in this. Certainly it must be true that a child who is inducted gradually into farm life, from an early age, is easier to oversee (and to motivate) than a teenager who is suddenly introduced to the farm. The principle would seem to be: *start them early* — when this is possible.

HOW CITY YOUTH FIND FARM WORK

Some youth take farm jobs to make money. Others go out to the farm for experience (or their parents send them). For others, these motives are mixed. Since there is some demand for farm experience, this gives an opportunity to the farmer who cannot afford to pay competitive wages — if he is a man who has the type of farm, and temperament, that can accommodate to unskilled youths.*

Farm labor as a strictly business transaction is handled by

*This might be better put in the female gender, since farmwives can take in girls as mothers' helpers, probably with fewer complications than in the male case. However it may be that the farmer is less aware of the need for female help.

state employment agencies and (in Canada) by Canada Manpower. In addition there is the informal network of friends and relatives by which farmers and youths find each other. If the youth is kin to the farmer, this softens the economic considerations; he is apt to be taken into the family. Then there are nonkin youth who are referred by relatives, and youth who are children of good friends, where something like a diluted kin obligation applies. In cases of this sort, I have several times found the boy or girl loafing. Evidently the farmer and his wife tried to include them in the work team; after some failures everyone gave up and the visitor — whose role may have been ambiguous to begin with — assumed the role of guest. Nevertheless, I have heard of city-cousin arrangements which were successful. The city cousin worked hard and came back the next summer. This is a traditional arrangement that goes back in our history. If farm experience came to be more valued, perhaps more city cousins would go to the farm. On the other hand, since working farms are diminishing year by year, ever fewer city people have country relatives to visit.[8]

There is also the status of the paying guest. Farms across Canada that belong to farm vacation associations take in tourists. These people usually come as families, I think, but some farms take in children and teenagers without their parents. I have heard of children who were sent to farm vacation homes with the expectation that they be put to work. Farm vacations should probably be lumped with various other short-term "exposure" experiences: well worth doing as experiences, but hardly work training. In this vein, I have heard of an exchange program that sends city youth to country homes, while their farm-youth counterparts visit homes in the city.

Farm vacations and country-cousin arrangements must usually be cases of children being sent, more or less, by their parents. If the youth actively wants and seeks farm experience, and finds it for himself, then the likelihood that he will work hard

---

[8]Hugh A. Blackmer, "Agricultural Transformation in a Regional System: A Study of Economic Development and Population Change in the Annapolis Valley, Nova Scotia" (Unpublished paper, Department of Anthropology, Stanford University, Stanford, California, 1972).

and get more benefit is probably greater. In this category, one could put devotees in a number of special interest groups. One such group is comprised of youth (mainly girls, I think) who are in love with horses. They have information networks that get them jobs and summer experiences at riding stables and horse farms and ranches. Some of these horse jobs actually entail hard work. The barn cleaning and grooming can offer, I would think, some hardening (of a sort) and work training, and the girls are probably emulating adult models.

A second group is the people who are interested in homesteading. At the time of this writing, *The Mother Earth News* runs about fifteen pages per issue of a personals column, for people trying to get together in homesteading ventures. Homesteading demands the cultivation of survival skills, and it offers a return to basic chores. It does not help the farmer with his work, but it looks like a hopeful development for giving farm-type training to young people.

A final arrangement is: the city family moves to the country or to a small rural community. The father commutes to work; or perhaps he has retired; or maybe they are only summer people. This group blends with the homesteaders. Some of these people live on farms and take on various agricultural enterprises; there is work to be done, and the children may be drawn into it. But since they are not traditional farmers, and are less constrained by necessity pressure, their children probably work less than born-and-bred farm children. Still, rural living may teach mechanical and self-maintenance skills, and adaptibility to primitive conditions — even if it is somewhat diluted in these sorts of arrangements.

Chapter 5

MODELING, EMULATING

MICHAEL AT THE AGE OF READINESS

TO repeat: children at age three or earlier show an interest in adults' activities. They want to watch what the adults do, and they copy some of it in their play. They want to help. If simple tasks can be given the child, then an apprenticeship can unfold. Helping, participating, and watching, the child can model after the parent.

In the primitive villages, this was usually possible. Conditions of life meshed with the child's natural inclinations. In our situation, this is seldom possible. Few homes provide children a series of tasks appropriate to their age and start them on this line of development. At a somewhat older age, some farm families, large families, and families that live in unmodernized homes can give a work-apprenticeship. But most parents must watch this period of readiness come and go and do little or nothing about it.

I have watched my own child developing and I have worried about this. When Michael was three, after we got a television set, the imitative behavior appeared. His imaginary play began to incorporate Spiderman and the other characters and monsters from the TV cartoons. He dressed as a cowboy. He galloped back and forth through the house on a horse made from a broomstick. Sometimes he was a policeman and other times he was a fireman.

The cowboy, fireman, and policeman evidently represented Michael's earliest ambitions. At various times, he has said that he would grow up to be a cowboy, a fireman, or a policeman. The role models came mainly from television, I think, and secondarily from children's books.

At age three, Michael also began to pester his mother in the kitchen. He wanted to join in and "help." She was terribly patient with him and invented small things he could do to participate in her baking, or cleaning, or (later) gardening work. But he was an awful pest. We had nothing constructive that a three-year-old could do (such as carry in firewood). Also note: he was trying to help his mother, not me. Why? Because he never saw me doing any work. I work at a typewriter. I exhibit no work behavior that could be copied or that would excite any interest.

Michael is now five. He has spent the past two years shooting guns, riding his horse around the house, and playing imaginary games with make-believe characters. When he plays with a friend, they both do this — improvising little dramas that must have been inspired by television. He also continues to "help" his mother in ways that tend to be inappropriate and bothersome.

It is a bizarre situation. This natural human inclination has blossomed forth at the appropriate age. He is ready and eager to begin on his apprenticeship, but the setting for it no longer exists. There are no errands to be run, no tools to be fetched or held, father or uncle or elder brother to be followed around as they work, no work team of older children and adults. So the models that he imitates come from television, and he gallops around the house on a horse made out of a broomstick.

John Marshall's film on the Bushmen of South Africa, *The Hunters,* shows little boys playing at hunting, shooting their bows and arrows, preparing for the real thing. Humans evolved in hunting bands such as those of the Bushmen. Shooting, hunting, and killing seem to be intrinsically interesting to little boys. Their imaginations are fired by dangerous, violent, male pursuits: pilot, fireman, warrior.

The traditional Nova Scotian occupation of fisherman has something of this romantic aura. In Moose Harbor, Blue Rocks, Lunenburg, other coastal towns, the marine outfitters sell rubber boots of all sizes. Little boys clump around in boots identical to the fishermen's.

Children are also interested in animals and animal care; and they show interest in machines. When I began to take Michael with me on my visits to farms, he was fascinated. He wanted to stay. There were the animals — cows in the barn, a horse perhaps, maybe chickens. The farmer would be doing things with noisy motorized equipment: a chain saw, a milking machine, a tractor. The first farm scene he ever witnessed was a farmer with a teenage helper, cutting fence posts with a chain saw. Michael said, "I want to be a farmer."

Other adult activities, such as the mother's work around the house, may have somewhat less intrinsic fascination. But children can develop strong interest in these, too, if they can watch them; especially so, if they can participate. The bare minimum requirement must be that the activity is physical, and not abstract, paper and pencil. Children can comprehend little of office work activities until they are practically grown. Those of us who work in offices really have nothing to offer our children along these lines, other than what we do when we are not working.

I will give an example of this. I have a friend who is a clinical psychologist. He has always carried a heavy work load. He now has the equivalent of three jobs in a large mental hospital. He is the director of the research and evaluation department, and he sees patients. Either of these positions — hospital administrator or psychotherapist — is a stressful job. He does both, and he also works on his own research. The story is: he thought he would take his twelve-year-old son, Ricky, to the office with him, to show him where his father went off to when he left the house for work every day. Ricky sat in the office through a number of conferences and hung around through about half a day's work. And what was Ricky's reaction to all this? He thought his father had a really good job. From what he could see, his father just sat around and drank coffee, and read for awhile, and then he talked to someone for awhile, and then he drank some more coffee, and talked to someone else, and then he drove home from work. (The driving home part — Ricky could actually see this.)

Our own children go through a series of personal ambitions, want-to-be-likes: a fireman, policeman and so on; to (later) emulating teenage idols (the ego ideal might be a glamour-girl type, for girls, and maybe an athlete type, for boys) . . . to finally wanting to be like some great success, some admired figure, in the occupation one chooses. Also, along the way, one may wish to be like particular people who excel in this or that, or whom one especially admires.

In the primitive villages, there must have been less variety in whom children emulated. If the early childhood interest was harnessed in a work-apprenticeship, so that the boy was working for his father (or other older male role models) and the girl was working with her mother (or other older females), then there should have been a better chance for a straight-line development: Emulation of early role models might continue as the child matures.

I think some girls still do develop this way. Their early role modeling, in the home, has been less interfered with (as a result of modern conditions) than has boys'. A number of the girls in my sample tell stories that sound like this: a straight-line development from early-childhood interests, wanting to be like mother and wanting to participate in her work, to mother's helper, child-care duties, baby-sitting jobs, an ambition to be a mother herself, or a nurse or teacher, and finally a realization of that goal. I will be describing one of these cases.

For fathers and sons there is less opportunity for this. Copying after the father, wanting to be like him, and comparing oneself with him may be a continuing theme in the boy's life. The impress of the father may be powerful, even in the absence of a work-apprenticeship. But the line of development is different. It is not a straight-line development into a lifework and an occupational self. If the boy and his father seldom work together, but rather play together and do other things together, then the outcome of role modeling must be somewhat different. Later I will tell the story of Jerry, who apprenticed to his father in hobbies.

A CAPE BRETON FISHING VILLAGE

This village represents a traditional way of life — now on its way to extinction — that did offer a work-apprenticeship to boys. Gerard, who grew up there, went through all the classic stages — hanging around the boats, watching, listening to the fishermen's stories, playing at it, being eager to go out to sea himself, then finally getting his chance, going through an apprenticeship, and at last having his own boat and lobsterman's license. As the apprenticeship changed from play to work, a sobering realization slowly dawned — of the terrible hardships involved, the risks, the limited opportunity, even the drudgery. Today he would like to go back to his home on vacation, and perhaps fish as a hobby, but he has decided that it is not a feasible lifework. He sounds like some farm boys whom I have talked to. They also must have gone through an early period of eagerness, then a later awakening to the poor prospects of farming for making a livelihood.

Gerard's Story

"As soon as we children were old enough to run through the fields and down to the beach, we watched the boats. We argued about which boat was the fastest, which fisherman was the best. Our make-believe games were pretend fishing, navigating boats, and putting out nets. We would take a cart or a riding sleigh and deck it out with ropes, buoys, crates, and other gear for a fishing trip. We built little toy boats out of scrap wood, and sailed them on ponds and on puddles. We got model boat kits for presents.

"When I was twelve I converted a two-foot-deep windowsill into a boat that would carry me. At first it leaked, but I covered it with plastic. My mother warned me not to try to sail it. But I did try. The official launching was at a nearby pond. My friends watching, I paddled around for about five minutes. Then I made a wrong move, and I capsized.

"During the long winters I watched my grandfather knit headings, make lobster traps, and ready his gear for the coming season. He and the other men, while they worked, would tell fishing stories. From listening to this talk we children learned many things about going out to sea. We also participated in painting boats and buoys and catching bait.

"I began going out in the boats when I was maybe eight years old. My grandfather and uncle would take me along with them. On the same day, my friends might be going out with their folks. I got much more interested in fishing. Pretty soon, we could actually do some of the work; we began hiring out to other fishermen.

"People around home say that wanting to fish and be on the water 'gets in your blood.' It certainly did for me. But my mother made it plain that I could not drop out of school.

"I found an old lobster trap on the beach. It became my trap. I would go out with my father, help him pull up his traps, set them, and bait them. My share would be whatever was in my own trap. I accumulated more traps. Pretty soon I had ten or fifteen traps. They provided nice income for a young boy.

"When I was thirteen I bought an outboard motor on credit. I put it on my father's rowboat. I could now go out by myself and tend my own traps. Since the motor had to be paid for, I needed more traps. I repaired old traps, built new traps with my father's help. Gradually, fishing for fun changed to fishing as a business. I built up my lobstering during the summertime season. Off season, I went to school and did other things."

Gerard says that as a child he had to beg and plead to be allowed to accompany the men and older boys on a fishing trip. His mother opposed it, saying it was dangerous. That made him want to go out all the more. As he grew older and actually became useful in the boat, the men wanted him to go along. They began to ask him to go every day. Then he went out in bad weather (which off the Cape Breton coast can be fearsome), as well as good.

Fishing began to be a chore the year he started helping his father with the salmon nets and mackerel nets, getting up before dawn each morning. When he was obligated to do it, every day, the fun aspect began to disappear.

When Gerard had his own traps to tend, he had to go to them too every day, fair weather or foul. He had trouble with his motor, lost gear in storms, and suffered some financial reverses. Gerard says it gets harder as you get deeper into it: more lobster traps, more investment, more time spent, and more work. "By the time I finished high school I knew enough about commercial fishing to know I didn't want to make it my main source of income."

Lynn

Lynn modeled after her mother and her older sister, helping in her home as a child and later as a teenager in other homes. Hers is but one of several dozen such cases that I have in my collection. Making allowance for a bit of idealization, perhaps, in the story, all the ingredients appear to be here: early imitation and play at helping soon turning into real housework and child care, under a mother who provided good teaching and example; genuine need for Lynn's help; and a step-wise progression to more responsibility and heavier work load as Lynn got older.

"My mother says that when I was three years old, I would follow her around while she was dusting. I touched the chairs in imitation of her dusting movements. I imitated other work she did in this way. I know what she means, because I have seen children I baby-sat imitating me.

"From the time I was small, I and my older sister were needed to help out. We had younger brothers and another younger sister. The children came at fairly close intervals. The amount of work increased, and my mother had less and less time.

"The three of us worked together. My mother told us what had to be done and supervised us. I was particularly eager to help with baking. I remember my mother as being willing and patient in showing me the right way to do things. She was especially cautious in teaching me how to care for a baby. She let me do a little at a time, and watched me, and gradually let me do more.

"Along with my mother, I had another example to follow in my older sister. She has always been responsible and mature for her age, even as a child. Mother was in and out of the hospital a lot. When that happened my sister took charge. I remember when she was eleven and I was nine. She did everything my mother would do: cooking, cleaning, washing, and taking care of the young children. She handled these jobs better than anyone would have expected.

"Everyone in my family thinks a lot of my sister; especially my mother does. She was better at these tasks than I was. She set an example that was difficult to follow. She is wonderful with children; she has been since she was very young herself. She could anticipate what a child needed and wanted; and she could attend to him physically; and she was very patient and understanding with their fussings. So all the children love her. We have always been in competition, and she has always been better. I tried to imitate her."

Other people in my sample who had paragon elder sisters withdrew from the competition and refused to work. Ann and Brent (in later chapters) reacted this way. Depending on other factors in the situation, sibling competition can spur ambition and effort, or it can have the opposite effect.

Lynn then goes on to describe her child-care career; first caring for her own brothers and sister and later working in other homes.

"The most demanding job I had was looking after three-week-old twins while their mother was in hospital. I lived in and was in charge of the house. Also there was a four-year-old daughter who was quite spoiled and unused to having two crying babies around. I found it difficult to plan my household duties around the babies' schedule, because, unlike one baby, twins require much more attention. It was strenuous at the beginning, but as I became better acquainted with the schedule, things began to run more smoothly."

She has also had several other mother's helper jobs and has cared similarly for an old woman. She feels she is now pretty good at the job and that she has the requisite maternal-nurturant disposition; she looks forward to becoming a mother herself.

Lynn seems to have had ideal home conditions for learning the mother role. Curiously, other girls developed much the same way, *without* these good conditions. Several girls in the sample who had no younger siblings, no babies to practice on, showed a keen and unflagging maternal "instinct" from an early age. They went out and searched for younger children to nurture, visiting and helping in neighbors' homes, perhaps seizing upon an infant cousin or nephew; playing a maternal role in a neighborhood play group; and finally doing it for pay. They have had a maternal career throughout their childhood and teenage years. Their dispositions are what one would expect, as a result of a successful apprenticeship. But whatever apprenticeship they had, they found for themselves in other homes. Therefore, I must conclude that the good start, within the home, must facilitate this kind of development. But it does not seem to be absolutely necessary; at least not for some girls.

MODELING VIA NONWORK

What about the children whose home duties are trivial and take up little time, who seldom work alongside the parents? The parents' influence, such as it is, must be transmitted during nonwork activities. Can any substitute activities take the place of a work-apprenticeship? At times, I think certain hobbies and leisure pursuits can be a partial substitute.

I have arranged possible leisure activities on a scale. Just what the scale represents is not completely clear in my mind. It has to do with the complexity of the activity and how much is required in the way of planning, arrangements, and social adjustments. Activities that are high on the scale are approaching the realm of joint work and responsibility training. Here is the scale, starting with the low points:

1. Household leisure time: watching TV, eating meals. The parent chauffeurs the child to and from various places.

2. Stereotyped games: Ping-Pong, Chinese checkers, the classic competitive games and sports that are narrowly rule bound.

3. More complicated and less stereotyped sports and outings: going fishing and hunting; family travel.

4. Even more complicated ventures — canoe trips, camping — where there is equipment to manage, plans to lay, and an approach to something like a family work team.

4. or 5. Mechanical work: working on projects, parent and child together, fixing or making things.

Activities at higher points on the scale give a chance for the child to participate in a responsible way, do some of the work himself, and model after the working adult, if the child is old enough and if the parent will let him.

Leisure activities' potency, as media for role modeling, must depend on such factors as these:

- How much time parent and child spend together;
- This scale: Are they getting involved in projects that are quasi-work?
- How the parent behaves: Is he a good teacher? Is he skillful, effective?

I would like to quote, here, from the case of Jerry. Jerry's father must have been a very strong and effective role model. He is described as a free spirit — footloose, who finally left home for good when Jerry was fifteen. Last heard from, he was somewhere in the South Pacific, engaged in questionable business dealings. Jerry seems to have turned out much the same. He started long-distance hitchhiking and world traveling soon after his father left home, following his father's footsteps. He continues to care for his gun like his father taught him. He also gives the impression of setting high personal standards for himself, of a particular sort, reminiscent of his father's early teaching.

The father taught Jerry several of his hobbies. These served as a partial substitute for a work-apprenticeship. The father sounds like a good teacher.

"I spent a fair amount of my spare time with my father. He was a very strong willed and self-sufficient individual. He seemed capable of mastering any situation, and I always tried to copy him. Some of his interests which I became involved in were hunting, fishing, hand-loading ammunition and working with wood and leather. I would watch him when he was doing something and he would always explain what he was doing. He would let me help, teaching me step by step, until I was able to do the work alone. His standards were always very high, and I would try my hardest to be competent at what I was doing. My father did not attempt to direct my interests, but he always helped and encouraged me to be capable at what I tried to do. He would take me shooting with him, and when I was a good shot and responsible with a gun, he gave me my own rifle. I was twelve or thirteen at the time. My age never seemed to matter. I was always treated according to my capabilities."

The book *Changing Children's Behavior,* by John and Helen Krumboltz, talks about modeling in behaviorist terms. An effective parent is one who usually does the right thing — reinforces desirable behavior — in interactions with the child. The parent is the child's first model. He (or she) gets the first chance. "Parents are sometimes worried about their children falling under the influence of bad companions. However bad companions are a serious danger only if the good companions fail to provide the reinforcement needed by a child."[1]

Krumboltz and Krumboltz then talk about delinquent models leading children into delinquency; about role modeling not succeeding in certain cases where the parents are inadequate models; and about how powerful interests and work motivations can be instilled by certain parents and teachers who *are* effective models.

By *modeling,* they mean simply imitating someone: "Children imitate many other kinds of behavior in addition to speech patterns. The people whose behavior is imitated are called 'models.' . . . Modeling is frequently unintentional . . . *Modeling Principle: To teach a child a new way of behaving, allow him to observe a prestigeful person performing the desired behavior. . . .*

Adequate or inadequate models can influence a variety of behaviors."[2]

Role modeling, conceived in this way, means you imitate a model's behavior, and as a result you acquire behavior dispositions that tend to stay with you as you grow up.[3]

One can distinguish (1) the *opportunity* for role modeling from (2) the child's *modeling behavior.* There is also (3) its continuing effects into later life.

1. The optimal opportunity for role modeling would be an old-fashioned work apprenticeship. The model's activities can

---

[1]John D. Krumboltz and Helen B. Krumboltz, *Changing Children's Behavior* (Englewood Cliffs, New Jersey, Prentice-Hall, 1972), p. 54.
[2]Ibid., pp. 48-63.
[3]Dennis L. Krebs, "Altruism — An Examination of the Concept and a Review of the Literature," *Psychological Bulletin,* 73:267, 1973.

be observed and comprehended by the child; the child can practice some of this in play. Then the child begins to apprentice, doing some actual work. A good deal of the work is done in the model's actual presence and under her (or his) supervision.

2. Children's modeling behavior would include hanging around, being underfoot and in the way, watching adults' activities; offering to "help"; and then later imitating some of it in play. When the work-apprenticeship begins, the modeling behavior (wanting to be in on what the parent is doing and wanting to do what the parent does) would be showing willingness to do the work.

My central idea about role modeling is that the two processes — modeling and learning to work in the home — come together, and each one facilitates the other. At least, this is true when the home is such that something like the traditional work-apprenticeship is possible. I think there is a stage in life, starting at about the age of three, when the child is interested in what the adults are doing and wants to watch and help. If the learning-to-work process can begin during this period of readiness, and if it is not too badly mismanaged by the parent, then it all flows together. The child learns home-connected work, graduates to more mature responsibilities, is positively motivated in this area, and models after the parent.

3. Many possible effects of role modeling are mentioned in the psychological theories. One effect is the traces of the parent, the lasting influence, that the grown-up child carries with him. Another possible effect is continuing emulation of the parent, a carry-over of the early desire to imitate and be like the role model. In addition, there is continuing motivation to do the work.

If the combined processes of role modeling and learning-to-work are successful, then the outcome should be:

• An older child, teenager, young adult, who is a willing worker in the home, who retains his willingness to participate in the work and help;

• Who still wants to work alongside the parent;

• And who continues to want to do the sort of work around the home that was learned in childhood.

The reality of what actually happens must be more complicated than this schematic description of role modeling. Actual cases present apparent contradictions:

- A parent often seems to succeed with one child and fail with the next. A hardworking farm boy has a lazy brother, perhaps a helpful sister, and another lazy sister. An auto mechanic has one son who also wants to work on cars and another son who wants nothing to do with them.

- All kinds of contradictions are possible within the same child. A girl willingly helps her mother and is hardworking in the home, but she does not want to become a mother herself. A boy cannot work alongside his father; there is too much friction. Yet he seems to emulate his father and want to be like him (in certain respects); he may be interested in farming, or mechanics, or whatever his father's occupation is; and he may be a hard worker.

- Add to these contradictions changes in behavior over time. Some children's work behavior is erratic. Children may work well in one setting and not in another. In addition, as teenagers develop, they change, and there are many surprises. Ambitions change; old interests give way to new ones. Stages are passed through. A move to a new work situation calls forth new behavior. A girl who was "lazy" within her own home becomes a hard worker when she helps out in another home.

To sum up: role modeling can combine with learning to work in the home. The result is generally "good," I think, at least from the parent's point of view — a helpful, emulating offspring. But the case studies show instances of failure, too. They also show many contradictions.

Role modeling has to proceed as best it can without the benefit of a work-apprenticeship when there is no particular need for the child's help.

Just what is possible along these lines depends on whether the parent is a good teacher or a bad teacher. It also depends on whether there actually is work in the home that can serve as the medium for a work-apprenticeship. Surprisingly, grossly inept parents can get pretty good results, if the other conditions are favorable.

Chapter 6

FAILED MODELING,
TURNED-OFF APPRENTICES

THIS chapter is devoted to the failures. These are farm children, girls who were needed for child care and housework, and other children whose help was needed, who did not develop in the expected way. Some didn't like farm work or child care or whatever their work was. Some were "lazy." A few seemed to lack any helping impulse. Some disliked working with their parents. They contrast with the children who were willing helpers, keen to participate in the family's work, eager to work alongside the parent and model after him (or her). Their work-apprenticeships must have misfired because of parental mishandling or because of various unfortunate accidents. Some possible reasons for these failures will be given.

Children tend to assume specialized roles in the family. This is most noticeable in large families and on farms. There is the responsible and martyrish eldest child, the spoiled baby, the mechanical son, the bookish child, a son who takes after his father, the family scapegoat, a lazy child, and so on. This phenomenon — and what is behind it — will serve as an introduction to our subject. The anthropologist Jack Roberts explains it as follows:

Children tend to get typed early in life: bright, slow, responsible, flighty, a steady worker, talented at this or that, and so forth. On the basis of these imputed abilities they get different tasks assigned to them — some kids doing the mindless, routine jobs, others being given the more complicated and judgmental jobs. Evaluations of their performance tend to be colored by the same biases. For example if a child has been typed as irresponsible, then his irresponsible actions are more apt to be noticed and remembered. Therefore, whatever the children's original

65

inclinations, their development diverges along different tracks.[1]
Roberts' explanation then becomes more complicated; but this
will suffice for our discussion.

Any tendencies in this direction must be reinforced by different incentives and practice. For example, a farm boy who
gets defined as "mechanical" will have his early mechanical
efforts noticed, exclaimed over, and retold; he will get recognition and encouragement to do more; and he can see the importance of fixing things and the family contribution that it
represents. Positively motivated and interested, he spends time
on this, learning and progressing. In a short time, he should be
far ahead of another boy who was not tracked in this way.

Such an explanation puts the emphasis on getting a good
start — positive motivation at the beginning, interest, and early
practice. School successes and failures can be explained in the
same fashion. Learning to read, especially — whether it comes
quickly or slowly, easily or hard, pleasantly or unpleasantly —
can quickly separate the children. By third grade some children
will have read perhaps ten times the material that others have
read; they will be able to read more advanced material and read
with ease and pleasure. They will be typed as good students by
their teachers. They will be on their way to school success. Any
child who gets bogged down at the beginning stands in grave
danger of falling behind, not liking it, getting typed as slow,
and never doing well in school.

One can further explain children's differing roles in a family,
by pointing to forces operating within the family itself. For
example, certain families seem to need a scapegoat; so the
scapegoat role emerges in these families.[2] Sibling rivalry can
also result in specialized roles, I think. We will be reviewing a
case of this sort. Finally there is the necessity pressure principle. In large families, this must account for the hard working

---

[1]Professor John Roberts, Department of Anthropology, University of Pittsburgh:
personal communication. He is talking about children in a Guatemalan village who
were his research subjects; but what he says has wider applicability.
[2]Norman Bell and Ezra Vogel, "The Emotionally Disturbed Child as the Family
Scapegoat," *A Modern Introduction to the Family*, rev. ed. (New York, Free Press,
1968), pp. 412-427.

eldests and the "spoiled babies." As one informant from a large farm family said, of a younger sister who had only housework to do: "There were enough of us by then."

Turning now to the failure cases — the children who are not keen workers, not eager to pitch in and help, not seeming to emulate a parent — I have put them into four types. These should be taken for what they are, rather artificial categories, since most of these youths could be simultaneously put in two or more of the types; and at any rate the case material is none too reliable for purposes of this sort. The four types are (1) the youth who does not particularly like the farm work (or whatever) that he has to do; (2) the lazy kids; (3) the youth who is reluctant to help out, who seems morally deficient — of a sense of responsibility, or sympathy for the hardworking parent; and (4) the youth who dislikes working with his father.

1. One becomes aware of this type in visiting farm families: Some kids are enthusiastic about becoming farmers themselves, and seem to be emulating a parent; others will leave the farm. As far as one can divine their motives, there are all sorts of cases of mixed feelings, ambivalence, perhaps liking farm life but disliking work for the father, and so on, as well as simpler cases of hatred of farm work, and liking for it but with a preference for something else. Making allowance for realistic reasons for leaving the farm, and for the hardships of farm life and limited opportunity that might persuade a youth to take up a nonfarm career, I still assume that something went wrong in the apprenticeships. Other farm youth, with no more "realistic" encouragement (as far as one can tell), are keen to be farmers.

Some girls who served as their mothers' lieutenants say they do not want to have children themselves. (I am skeptical about this. They may feel this way now, but I would be surprised if most of them did not eventually become mothers.) Girls who are veteran housecleaners say it is a drag. (No doubt this is true, if you have to work by yourself.) Three girls in my sample who were older sisters, whose burden of child care, housework, and other work was especially heavy, are now rather embittered by their experience. They feel that their parents took advantage of them, although they admit the hardworking parents probably had no choice. Two of them say they now hate the disorder and noise of children in the house. But the third is a mother, and all three were yeoman workers and helpers (they say), as children and teenagers.

2. A second group which could be termed failures is the "lazy" kids. These must result from bad parental handling. Laziness will be taken up in later chapters, when I discuss willingness to work and work habits.

3. The next type of failure has to do with a deficiency of character rather than mere distaste for work. Actually, the distinction between this and laziness is rather academic. However, I wish to take account of the moral impulse that lies behind "pitching in" and "helping out." The term *sense of responsibility* comes close to describing it. The case that has best illustrated it is Virginia (in the *Child Care* chapter) who worked willingly to help her hard-pressed mother, fixing supper and cleaning the house so it would be ready when her mother came home from work, while her "lazy" brothers and sister and father refused to help. In a similar case, the mother runs an inn. There is a lot of work to do, and she needs the help of her four teenage and grown children. According to my informant, the mother may be up at 5 AM rushing to meet some deadline, while the kids sleep until noon. When they do help, they want to be paid. The informant, who herself was a farm girl, says she could never have stood idly by like that and not helped her mother.

These cases contrast sharply with the beautifully helpful farm children and large-family children whom I have seen. Why they were failures, we can only guess. Helpfulness, and how it can be taught or discouraged, is the subject of Chapter 8.

4. A final type of failure is the boy who dislikes working for his father (or girl for her mother). The apprenticeship, which must have begun with the little boy eager to watch, eager to tag along and to help, ends with avoidance. Often it is probably not this simple: There are both positive and negative elements in the relationship. Work with the father is attractive in some ways, aversive in others. The father, as a work master and model, does both good things and bad things. But the father-

son relationship is troubled: There is some estrangement, and this spills over into their work relationship. Or perhaps their overall relationship is not particularly disturbed, but the father simply does a bad job of managing the boy's work, so the son dislikes working for him.

What went wrong and how to account for these failures is part of the larger subject of instilling work motivation and helpfulness, the topic of following chapters. Some possible reasons for these failures that are suggested by the case material are as follows:

• The child was "held back," was not graduated up to more mature work and responsibility at an appropriate rate; this damaged his motivation.

• The parent was abusive; he nagged or belittled or unfairly blamed the child.

• Other family relationships interfered with the apprenticeship. I have found two varieties of these. In one, a child balks at work, evidently because of a sibling rivalry situation. In the other, the parents cannot cooperate, so that one parent's commands are countermanded by the other.

These will occupy us for the remainder of the chapter, along with two anomalies: Work within the family can make for solidarity, but it also is a reason for conflict; finally, these "reasons" do a poor job of explaining the failures, since they do not separate my success cases from the failure cases. Some of the keenest apprentices have parents who are obviously guilty of nagging or belittling, or various injustices, or parental noncooperation. Some of my most admirable farm youths and child nurses are so, despite what looks like serious family problems and mismanagement. I view these "reasons" merely as varieties of trouble that can occur in apprentice situations, which look like they should be affecting the outcome; and I think sometimes they do.

THE CHILD WAS "HELD BACK"

This is part of the more general autonomy struggle which is characteristic of adolescence — the child wanting more and more, the parent yielding control grudgingly or fearfully: the keys to the car, permission to stay out until 2 AM and do other grown-up things.

I will give two illustrations: first a good example, then a bad example. The case of Leo, the good example, is described in the Krumboltz book. Leo worked with his father in the yard. The father was a good and skillful teacher; he *did* graduate the boy up to more grown-up tasks when he seemed ready. As a result, Leo sometimes chose to work in the yard rather than go out with his friends. My bad example, Jim, is the grown son of a dynamic father who has built houses, bought and sold farms, and has gone into ventures which generally involved buying a property, fixing it up or building onto it, and then reselling. He has worked his sons hard. But while his projects could have enabled a superb education in fixing and farming and construction, he has tended to keep them at a little-boy stage of "Hand me that screwdriver" and "Run and get me the pliers." He oversupervised them, tended to keep them at routine tasks, and did not graduate them up — when they were ready — to more mature and interesting jobs. (This is of course an oversimplification of what must have happened.) Jim expresses considerable resentment at this. But he has been a faithful worker on the family work team. He looks like a brilliant success despite this particular abuse by the father.

In the primitive villages and in this culture, too, the first tasks asked of little children seem to be mainly fetch-and-carry: "Get me this" or "Hand me that." I have seen a number of dominating fathers make these demands on their grown children: "Get me my shoes", "Get me my cigarettes." If the child yields to these demands, he (or she) must feel demeaned.

A similar cause for resentment is being "on call" and "tied to the house," something that can happen to girls who have much housework and child-care duties. Nevertheless, all my cases who express resentment at having been "on call" seem to have been faithful household workers.

ABUSES BY THE PARENT

Leslie's father once was a mechanic in a Volkswagen garage.

Now he and Leslie have their own shed in back of their house, which is dedicated to Volkswagen repair. In a nearby woodlot they have their own little Volkswagen junkyard. Leslie, working on his dune buggy with the assistance of a neighbor boy, has verve and style; he makes car repair exciting. Enter his father, and his self-assurance wavers. The father is helpful — with his help the boys quickly have the car running — but he makes several belittling comments: "If he were only smart in school, too." "You mean you spent all that time and hadn't got it started yet?"

The belittling comments are evidently calculated (unconsciously) to take away the boy's self-assurance, and they succeed. Ever so subtly, Leslie has become a bit clumsy. I am reminded of worse cases I have seen, of a belittling father (or mother) and clumsy son (or daughter). The prototype of this is certain Negro servants of a bygone day. I think of my aunt directing Oscar, her yardman.

Although this father-son relationship is flawed, Leslie is still keen to do mechanical work — like his father, and with his father. He appears to be developing well and identifying strongly with his father. His younger brother, on the other hand, has gone in exactly the opposite direction. He avoids the shed, has no interest in mechanical work, and supposedly does not know one end of a screwdriver from another. I speculate: somehow this kind of abuse by the father turned the younger boy away from working with him, whereas with Leslie the more positive elements in the relationship prevailed. Possibly too the case is complicated by sibling comparisons, as with the case of Ann (below).

An example of scapegoating — a rather mild example — is the case of Richard, an especially admirable farm boy, one of the eldest in a family of eleven. Richard is said to lack confidence and to be backward in learning to operate the heavy machinery. He too is "clumsy" in certain situations. With his little brothers he is superb. With Richard in the role of top sergeant, the work in the barn runs smoothly. His father or his elder brother enters and "it all falls apart": The harmony of the work team gives way to delays, disagreements, and "fooling around." The nature of the tensions between Richard and these two was never clear to me. There was some tendency for them to blame him for things. Presumably this was related to his awkwardness in certain work situations. His father said Richard had an uncontrollable temper; this seemed to be part of Richard's scapegoat image. Nevertheless, despite the trouble, one could not rate Richard a failure of work socialization; I would have to classify him as a smashing success.

A final case of parental mishandling is Leonard, a teenager in a wealthy home, whose only chore is to empty the nineteen wastebaskets and garbage cans every Sunday. When his mother is out of town he does this with no problem. When she is home it is one of the things she nags him about. "Have you emptied the trash yet?" "Pretty soon." (Later) "You better empty the trash now." "In a minute." And he may never do it. It is one more issue — along with being on time for meals and for school and doing his homework — for her to nag, him to resist. The little chore of emptying the trash has become enmeshed in a larger interaction problem between mother and son, which has a history, going back to earlier years. Doing chores for some other adult — even living in another house — Leonard would probably do better.

There are intimations in the case studies that some youths work better for strangers than they do for their parents. Some parents take liberties with their own children. They treat teenagers like younger children and exhibit regressed behavior of their own. Old bad habits continue on from earlier childhood days; any work relationship gets encumbered with all this. An apprenticeship to a stranger — stripped of this baggage — must often stand a better chance for success. This is discussed in the next chapter on Housework.

One wonders about the peasant villages described by the anthropologists, in which the father is generally said to have been authoritarian. His abuses of the work master role must have been gross. Why is there so little mention of youthful rebellion or parent-youth conflict? Is the son too hopelessly submerged — in the authoritarian structure of traditional peasant society — to rise up and rebel? This is a mystery.

PARENTAL CONFLICT

I don't believe this next problem would have troubled the peasant father. Glenn is a highly skilled fixer and handyman. He says his own son cannot do anything like that. I asked why Glenn did not pass his mechanical abilities along to his son. He said the son was always a "mama's boy," and Opal intervened when he tried to get the boy to work around the home. Glenn: "Mow the grass today." Opal: "Oh, let him go on and play, it's Saturday." If this story is taken at face value, the parents disagreed about the appropriateness of work orders. The father's orders were undercut by the mother. So the father evidently quit trying, or perhaps he could not put together a coherent work program or demand enough of the son to get good results.

In the days of traditional families — patriarchal or otherwise — in which there was an agreed-upon sex division of labor, when the father had his work and his sphere of influence (which was mainly outside the house), when generally speaking girls worked for their mothers and boys worked for their fathers, it all must have been simpler. In our modern families, democratically organized with consensual decisions, with weak traditional guidelines, with less clear rules about sex roles, division of labor, child rearing, and supervision of the children — the daily and hourly *do's* and *don'ts* and *mays* and *may nots* put a great strain on cooperation between mother and father. Each little issue is problematic, is a potential cause for conflict, has to be decided jointly — often under the pressure of the moment (under harassment by a child who wanted to *do* something, and under the constraint of trying to be consistent). This is one reason why parenthood is hard on marriages. (Marital adjustment studies show that couples' satisfaction and happiness scores go down when they become parents, and then go up again after the children grow up and leave home.)[3] It

---

[3]Angus Campbell, "The American Way of Mating: Marriage *Sí*, Children Maybe," *Psychology Today*, May, *8*, No. 2:37-43, 1975.

Norval Glenn, "Psychological Well-being in the Post-parental Stage: Some Evidence from National Surveys," *Journal of Marriage and the Family*, 37:1, 1975.

also must undermine some attempts at work training, as in the case of Glenn and Opal.

Any work the child does in the home tends to add more problematic issues to be decided. It increases the potential for conflict — both between the parents and between parent and child. In other words, work within the family tends to cause trouble. The trouble can be minimized by routinizing the supervision. If there is one work-master and no appealing to the other parent, if — after the work has gone on for awhile — the supervision issues that can come up have been pretty well settled, then the trouble should be minimized.

SIBLING RIVALRY

Anne's mother had a stroke when Anne was a little girl. For awhile the house was run with the help of hired girls and various relatives. As Anne and her sister grew older, the burden of housework began shifting to them. The sister Martha, one year older than Anne, was a willing worker. She cooked, cleaned the house, and minded their baby brother. She also excelled in school and was generally admired and approved. The need for her help, which was created by her mother's disability, brought out the qualities which now must be familiar: "team player," "good sport," and "pitching in and helping out." Anne declined to play this role. It is said that a line could be drawn down the middle of their room: Martha's side tidy, Anne's side chaos. Martha can remember rushing about the house, preparing for Thanksgiving dinner, while Anne "sat in her bed" in the midst of her mess. Unfavorable comparisons of Anne with Martha were evidently made often, at school as well as at home.

So what is Anne doing today? She is the devoted mother of four, playing the mother role with a vengeance (according to the report) under difficult conditions. How to account for the apparent change in her character? Her training in child care, family coping and helping evidently came on a mother's helper job which she took during her last two years of high school. The mother she helped was disabled (like her own mother) with a heart condition; she had four or five children. Anne went there after school and helped until supper. Evidently in this home, freed from the comparison with Martha and from any other old family problems that might have held her down, she responded to the challenge like Martha had previously done. I would speculate that Anne's own home provided the example and original training for helping behavior, but her resentment at being compared with her sister kept it from coming out. In a similar family situation, minus her sister — out the behavior came!

Chapter 7

HOUSEWORK IN MODERNIZED HOMES

MANY homes have little need for the children's help. There is no farm to run, no young children to care for or woodbox to fill. In fact, many of these homes require little work from anybody. If the father is not a tinkerer, he may do little around the house. The mother's necessary kitchen work and housecleaning is minimized by appliances and by the efficient layout of the home. In such homes, the skimpy chores that are required of children seem trivial as role modeling or as work training. They also appear to clash with the normal flow of life in the home; they go against the grain.

A vignette: The family's teenage children are upstairs in their rooms — doing homework, or perhaps watching one of their television programs. The mother shouts up words to the effect: "Harry — empty the garbage when you take the dog out." "Karen — wash the dishes." In time, each child hurries down to do chores. One has the feeling that these arbitrary-seeming commands, breaking into the leisured routine of the home, must be resented in a way that really heavy work in a necessity-pressure home would not be resented.

Talking to such parents, one hears the familiar story of how the kids drag their feet at doing chores. It may be a superior youth who is hardworking at school, but he does his household duties grudgingly. Telling the youth that his help is needed — that necessary chores cannot be handled without him — does not seem to help. A psychiatrist's son, whose father needed his help on their extensive flower garden and yard, responded to this appeal with, "Why don't you hire a yardman like you used to?"

The basic reason why the children don't want to help must be: no necessity pressure. Not only is their help not really needed, but the leisured household style has its effect on the parents' behavior as work supervisors and as examples.

It is easier for a mother to do the chore herself than to train and supervise her child. Since the child's help is less needed, there is less incentive to go to all the trouble of making the child into a household worker. Also, in a leisured household routine the family is less apt, I think, to be working as a team on household tasks. Add the multiplier effect which the teenage peer group brings to this as to other parent-youth conflicts: "Our friends don't do it, so we don't think we ought to do it." Besides, "I can't stay and do that because I'm going out with my friends." Various after-school activities and homework are used as reasons for not working around the home. The parents themselves use these excuses for not demanding more housework of their children. And it is true: For children who really have to work — after-school activities suffer; homework may suffer too.

Why is it easier to get children to work on the farm? We have been over this before: Necessity pressure; the example of their friends and siblings, who are apt to be helping their parents; (the "our friends don't do it" argument works the other way); the farm family's working-together style and spirit. The family jointly does basic work and copes with daily emergencies. Finally, in farm families, solidarity and parental control is supposedly greater.[1]

A "natural" learning-to-work sequence, such as we reviewed for the primitive villages or for farms — in which a child starts at about age three, watching older people in their work, following them around, imitating them, and then begins helping, with tasks appropriate to his age — chances for this are curtailed in a modern home. There are not a lot of people to watch and imitate. If the child is housebound much of the time (due to urban living conditions or a northern climate), the mother may be the only worker that can be observed. When it comes time to introduce a three-or four-year-old to household chores, it is hard to find tasks that are not too grown-up. Housework in modern homes tends to be fussy. Delicacy of handling and

---

[1]Pitrim A. Sorokin, Carl C. Zimmerman, and Charles J. Galpin, "The Family as a Basic Institution and Familism as the Fundamental Relationship of Rural Social Organization," *Systematic Sourcebook in Rural Sociology*, vol. 2 (Minneapolis, University of Minnesota Press, n.d.).

some maturity of judgment is required for nearly all tasks of any consequence. So it is difficult for a little child to be genuinely helpful.

Then what should a modern parent do? Give up and stop trying? That is one alternative, although there are several other alternatives that may be feasible. If the work relationship is going badly, as with the case of Leonard in the previous chapter, then giving up is probably not a bad idea. The youth might get a fresh start working with another adult outside the home. Or more feasible work socialization might come by way of a hobby or interest group, such as will be described in Chapter 11. If it is any consolation — and for whatever it is worth — the Whitings in their Six Culture Study found that housecleaning was least correlated with helpfulness and responsibility. It was the life-giving work that seemed to make the difference — bringing in and preparing the food and caring for babies.

Even if the child develops badly as a helper around the house, he may develop well in other areas. (This is said as further consolation, for parents who have failed in their attempts to get their children to help.) He may still turn out to be a hard worker at school, or at projects of his own. This kind of work may not be training in helpfulness, but it has its own value.

Working on projects can take the place of working at chores. Chores are the maintenance tasks: wash the dishes, empty the garbage, milk the cow, and slop the hogs. Someone has to do it. It is never ending and monotonous. Its burden may be lightened by the knowledge that you are thereby sustaining the family. And some chores are made sociable — the family does the work together.

Projects on the other hand involve making things and fixing things. They are problem solving and (in a humble way, perhaps) creative. They are generally interesting to whomever is working on them. Modern youth — and adults, for that matter — can take up innumerable hobbies and interests that are, in effect, "careers" of working on projects of particular sorts. The teenage hobbies tend to be self-centered. They are not training in helping, as farm work can be, or child care or basic home-maintenance work. However fixing and making things can go on in the home. The two kinds of work — working on projects and working for the family — can merge.

> Ursula, at age seven, is not only a helper; she is also interested in mechanical work. She showed an interest at an early age. When she was in nursery school she always wanted to hammer and saw. Her father works on repair jobs around the house, and Ursie watches and helps.

In some homes this is the family's style; in others it is not. Some fathers are household handymen. They are perpetually fixing or restoring or adding on to their home. They may be working on an outbuilding or on various yard projects. They repair the family automobile and other machines and appliances. They may have power tools in the basement. Such fathers can draw their sons into their work, as apprentices. I even know a few girls who apprenticed to their fathers in mechanical work.

The wife's projects may revolve around the garden and putting up the produce in the freezer and in Mason® jars. One might include cooking, too, when it is not too routinized. This can be combined with various crafts, and with cooperative husband-wife projects, fixing up the home.

I think this is most common in small communities and in the country. Perhaps it is least characteristic of middle-class and upper-class urban homes. However I have visited a few homes of professors and other professional people, in which family members worked together on one household project after another. This is probably the closest approximation, in modern urban homes, of the we-working-together family team, and the modeling through work, of the farms and primitive villages.

When the parents are themselves working hard around the home — at chores or projects — then there is something to base a work-apprenticeship on. There may be some limitations. Fussy and delicate work may delay a child's real participation. Lack of need for the children's help may diminish the significance of the work to them. And some parents will botch the job. But at least there is something to work with.

If the father is not a handyman — if there are few projects *or* chores to be done — *then* what should the parents do? Two other alternatives are open: (1) If a mother is a sufficiently good teacher, she can transcend her unpromising situation in a modernized home and train her children to be helpers. We will turn to these cases at the end of the chapter. (2) A child can learn to be a helper in someone else's home.

PLACEMENTS IN OTHER HOMES

Training in housework, child care, handyman work, and farm work is available in other homes. Some children will eventually find this for themselves; or the parents can take the initiative. They can arrange a series of placements, over a number of summer vacations — in other homes, where the work is going on, and where help is actually needed. They might start by taking advantage of what is available in the neighborhood or with relatives. As with any other arrangement for the children, they would try to find nice people who would provide good examples and good influences. They would hope to choose an adult who would be a good teacher and role model; and they should try to find an adult who actively *wanted* to talk to a child and teach him.

Some children will have already made a beginning. The parents need merely follow it up. The child may be especially fond of a certain grandfather or uncle, or habitually hangs out at a neighbor's house, or is fascinated by machines and mechanical work. Some little girls cannot wait to play mother to a younger child.

Some placements for younger children are:

• Visiting an old man who is a putterer. The child follows him around, watches, listens, and "helps" as he works in the yard and in his basement.

• Visiting a family that is working fairly hard on their home: fixing, maintaining it, maybe building onto it. Perhaps it is a big, old house, or a home in the country.

• Beginning child care: entertaining a younger child, under the parent's supervision. This is perhaps the type of work-apprenticeship that is most likely to be initiated by the child herself. I know of a number of little girls who went into neighbors' homes and volunteered their services. More commonly, a girl simply plays with younger children in the neighborhood, but she relates to them in a motherly fashion.

As children grow older they find paid baby-sitting jobs for themselves. Baby-sitting that includes housework is probably the best training. The ultimate is the mother's helper job, available to girls in their late teenage years.

Farm placements for children are harder to arrange. Some families have relatives or friends who live on farms. A few enterprising parents will search out good farm placements. I know a social worker who located a French Canadian farm that had been a foster home; she arranged for her own children to spend their summers there. If a full-fledged working farm cannot be found, a country home with a few farm activities might be a substitute. (With a garden, a few animals, fixing and maintenance work, berry picking, and so on.)

In many cases, more than one type of work can be learned in the same household: mechanical work and farm tasks; child care and housework; child care, housework, and farm tasks; or all four in one placement. If the placement involves staying overnight with the family, this probably intensifies the experience and makes it more "maturing."

I have several teenagers in my sample who became so attached to a childhood placement, on a farm or caring for a family of children, that they voluntarily went back to it, year after year. Others will want to try something new. As a child becomes older, he has a greater say in the decision about what he will do in his summer vacations. By the late high school years, the range of choice opens up enormously: paid jobs, travel opportunities, organized programs, and informal arrangements with friends; not to mention local hobby activities and enterprises of one's own.

Can working outside the home really take the place of helping out in one's own family? Can the helpful qualities be learned, working for someone else? Possibly, to some degree.

Children are certainly willing enough to be helpful in another home. As Dr. Spock observes, a task that is ordinarily done grudgingly for the parents may be done eagerly for someone else.[2]

But will these brief relationships, with strangers, have the same impact as the long-term relationship with the parents? We don't know.

When the child gets old enough to work for pay, this may introduce complications. There is research evidence that getting paid — under certain conditions — undermines motivation.[3] An enduringly helpful disposition is perhaps less effectively nurtured when the work is for pay; or perhaps, for many cases, it does not matter. Perhaps there should be a period of early household helping in childhood without pay. If helpful tendencies are started in childhood, with work within the home, then they can be developed and built upon, in later paid jobs such as mother's helper and hospital work.

Another question is: How early should such work begin, to produce helpful and responsible children? If the parents wait for the child to become a teenager and make his own arrangements, they may have waited too long and let the critical period, the age of readiness, go by. Here, too, we do not know the answer. People can, of course, learn housework skills later in life. The danger is that the underlying motivation, the helping need disposition, might not be the same.

Placing one's child in another home is unconventional. Conventional parents would keep their child home until his friends started going to camp; then they might send him to camp too. As he grows into his teenage years, he would eventually seek his own summer jobs and summer travels.

Sometimes the placement of a child happens so easily and naturally that it demands little of the parents. The child simply wanders over to a neighbor's house, or he visits a relative. Otherwise, the parents have to exercise initiative. They must

---

[2]Benjamin Spock, *Problems of Parents* (New York, Fawcett World Library, 1962), p. 49.
[3]Edward L. Deci, "Work: Who Does Not Like It and Why," *Psychology Today*, August, *6*, No. 3: 1972.

David Greene and Mark R. Lepper, "How to Turn Play Into Work," *Psychology Today*, September, *8*, No. 4:49-54, 1974.

seek out a farm vacation home (or whatever); they have to investigate it as best they can, and probably they must pay the people to take their child and make him work. Most parents would not do this. If the placement requires a young child to live in another home, there is all the more resistance. However I do know a few exceptional parents who were willing to undertake this, even for fairly young children. There is perhaps a need for a clearinghouse to bring parents and placement families together. School guidance offices, government employment offices, or learning exchanges* might perform this function, as various of them do now for teenagers' employment and summer activities.

What are the constraints which keep most parents from going this far? These are my guesses:

• It takes special effort and initiative. If the family is willing to consider letting the child leave home, they are more likely to send him to camp. There is an easy, established procedure for camp, all the easier if his friends are also going.

• Some parents do not want to impose on a neighbor or a relative or stranger. They hesitate to "be beholden" to someone else for training and supervising their child. Should some kind of payment be arranged? This might cause hesitation on both sides.

• The farmer or neighbor (or whoever) who took on a child might be legally liable if the child is injured. I do not believe that this is a serious obstacle. The parent could always sign a waiver. But it may be one more reason for people to hesitate at such an arrangement (or possibly it rarely enters anyone's mind; I do not know).

• When parents might finally be mobilized to act because they are alarmed about their child's development, by then it may be too late. The child is too old to be "placed" by then; he

---

*A learning exchange is a clearinghouse for individualized instruction and apprenticing. It keeps a card file of people who are willing to teach various things. Persons who want to learn can look in the file for subjects in which they are interested. Some major exchanges are: The DeKalb Learning Exchange, 633 West Locust, DeKalb, Illinois 60115; Binghamton Learning Exchange, P.O. Box 862, Binghamton, New York 13902; and The Learning Exchange, P.O. Box 920, Evanston, Illinois 60204, which lists over 2,500 subjects and skills to be taught.

is a teenager, and he has his own ideas about what he wants to do with his summers and weekends.

TESTIMONIES: A MODERNIZED HOME IS A POOR SETTING FOR TRAINING A CHILD TO BE HELPFUL

People disagree about this. Several mothers have told me that there is plenty of work in modernized homes and no lack of chores to give to the children. And for their own homes this is probably true. One of these mothers is a meticulous housekeeper; another is a fine cook. Meal preparation in a modernized home can be elaborate and time consuming, or simple and easy, depending on the cook's standards and style. The same is true for housekeeping and yard work. So I am sure that some housewives, with all the modern conveniences, continue to be hard working, even somewhat hard-pressed. Depending on their persistence and skill with their children, the kids may be drawn into this work.

On the other hand, I can cite a number of before-and-after comparisons. A country family moves to the city, and the family work team falls apart. A city family moves to the country, and the children become helpers for the first time. African villagers move to the city; old helping patterns disappear. The before-and-after comparisons imply that there is something in the urban home situation that discourages helping. (This is especially so, if there are no babies to care for, few household fixing projects, and the modern laborsavers.) Some parents transcend their poor situation and *still* get their children to be helpers; but many others do not.

> "Through my personal experience of moving from the city to the country, I can easily understand and agree with what you say about the pressure of necessity. At the age of twelve, living in the city, I contributed very little to the running of our household. If I was asked to do a job I usually did it grudgingly and after being asked more than once. I also used the argument, "Why should I have to do it, my friends don't do it.'
>
> "This changed when we moved to the country. There was

so much to do, it was obvious that everyone had to help out. [The family moved into an old farmhouse that had to be fixed up and renovated.] I even got interested in it — especially the construction work. I often helped out without being asked — something I'm sure I never did when we lived in the city. One more thing. In the country, my friends also had their chores to do. So my old argument, 'My friends don't do it,' lost its validity."

This was a Halifax family that moved to the country. Another case, a family that lived in Halifax, kept a country home — a primitive cottage — to which they returned every summer. There was no electricity in the cottage, water had to be carried, cooking and heating was by wood stove, and plumbing was nonexistent. While my informant, Mary, was growing up, they did this for sixteen summers. Mary was struck by how the yearly move to the country changed family life. First of all, everybody had to work much harder. Essential chores had to be performed daily: bringing in firewood, tending the stove, working in the kitchen, housecleaning (which was more difficult and time consuming than it had been in their city home), and so on. "Many times after we had finished cleaning, it looked like we had hardly touched it."

People's work had to be coordinated. The family, of necessity, worked as a team. They often worked together in groups.

"Each person had a very specific role that he had to play in order for it to function effectively. [For example, if the water carrier did not bring in water when it was needed or the wood carrier bring in wood, then other functions could not be performed.] It was essential that everything had to be carried out in an organized manner. . . . It is different when you are living in a city. If things aren't done in an orderly manner, then it does not really matter because there are so many things around you that can make up for it."

Mary cites the example of grocery shopping. In their country home, going to the grocery was a long trip; it was done once a week. They could not afford to forget anything, so the shopping trip was planned with some care. In the city, they could always go back to the store for something they forgot the first time.

When the family returned to the city in the fall, maintaining the household became easier again, and people lapsed back into their lazy and less efficient routines. The chores no longer drew them together. The children returned to school and went out with their friends. Family members led their own lives, went their separate ways.

In a third case, Kent describes his childhood in a big, old house on the outskirts of New Glasgow, Nova Scotia. There was a lot of fixing, building, and maintenance work. He and his brother were drawn into this at an early age. The family worked together on a variety of projects. When Kent was in the fifth grade the family moved to a city apartment in Halifax. Kent by this time had become a helper and a hard worker. The move to the city did not change this. When his mother got a job, he did the family's cooking. However the move to the city drew the family members apart. There was no place for a workshop.

> "Moving from a big house and having helped Dad a lot with the work, and then moving into a small flat, had its effects on our family. Dad and I lost touch with each other at this point for we had nothing in common to communicate on. You couldn't do any work on the flats together.
>
> "When we moved to a new flat on Jubilee Road, I adopted the Daniel family around the corner. . . . There were chores to do around the house, and there were lots of kids around. I also helped Donnie a lot in his school work. Even though I did spend a lot of time there I still went home to fix supper and clean up the kitchen afterward.
>
> "By now our family had separated completely and we each turned to ourselves for whatever we wanted to do. We were always out doing something on our own."

In Kent's case, the move to the city seems not to have undermined his helping tendencies; but it did destroy the family's working-together life-style.

A final before-and-after illustration comes from the Whitings' research in Africa. They followed some of their villagers who had moved to Nairobi, visited them in their shacktown dwellings, and applied the same behavior observation codes they had used on the village children. Thomas Weisner, a student of the Whitings who did much of this research, notes some of the differences between city life and village life:

- There were fewer chores for the children. (City amenities like running water and charcoal for fires had eliminated much traditional children's work.)
- The chores that children did were less critical, had less to do with life-giving work, and were more in the nature of errand-running and housekeeping.
- The routine of chores that must be performed every day, which is characteristic of country life both in Africa and here in North America, had given way to irregular, sporadic work (such as errands to run).

In analyzing the behavior observations, for the city children as compared with children in the villages, Weisner notes a large increase in "seeking behavior." *Seeking* includes asking for help, seeking attention, seeking comfort, and asking for food. Helpful behavior seems to have declined.[4]

TESTIMONIES: A MODERNIZED HOME IS *NOT* A POOR SETTING FOR
TRAINING A CHILD TO BE HELPFUL

A number of mothers have disagreed with my claim that there is not enough work for the children to do in modernized homes.

> "There is a lot they can do. At three, Michael helped with setting the table. By four he was picking up his toys and helping to tidy his room. He was doing things in the kitchen with me. He had helped me bake cookies and rolls by the time he was four. He had been with us when we worked in the garden."

The gist of the counter-argument goes as follows: Some housewives work very hard (because they are meticulous housekeepers, or they have a big yard, or whatever); others do not.

---

[4]Thomas S. Weisner, "The Child as Rural-Urban Commuter: Aspects of Socialization in City and Country Environments in Kenya" (Unpublished paper, Department of Anthropology, University of Calfornia at Los Angeles).

Beatrice B. Whiting, "The Effect of Urbanization on the Behavior of Children" (Unpublished paper, Cambridge, Harvard University).

However, someone has to do some work around the house — kitchen work and meal preparation, tidying up, and so on. A little child sees his mother doing housework, follows her around, and wants to participate. The child's original attitude toward housework must be positive. If the mother does not ruin it, it will stay positive, and the child will grow up into a helper. The trick is to harness the original interest.

In some homes, traditional sex typing bars little boys from housework. But this is a self-imposed limitation that does not have to be. In other families the father also works in the home, and he provides another role model.

Cooking, setting and clearing the table, washing dishes, all the work that goes on in the kitchen — this has to be done in all homes. One can argue that it should provide a fine training ground. There is a graduated series of tasks appropriate to the child's age. A three-year-old can play at "helping" his mother, then actually set the table, and go on to more grown-up work. A fairly young child can actually do a little cooking and get recognition for this. Kitchen work has a number of favorable characteristics for encouraging positive motivation to help. It is easily done in teams (working alongside mother, as opposed to working alone). Everyone's help is apt to be needed to some extent. As the cook brings the food to the table, there is sharp and instant appreciation. It is nurturance training, or it can be: You are feeding the family and being rewarded by their gratitude.

In addition to meal preparation, there are other opportunities to draw the children into work, depending on what needs to be done around the home.

If this is true, then why do most children in these homes do so little work, and do their few chores unwillingly? This question can be answered in about three different ways.

• There is the familiar recitation of reasons: little necessity pressure; a leisured household style, not much in the way of family work teams and positive example from other family members; "Our friends don't do it"; fussy and delicate housework; fewer tasks appropriate for a small child.

• Whatever the reasons, there seems to be a clear-cut difference between modernized homes (on the one hand) and unmodernized homes, farms, and other homes in which there is *really* a lot of work to be done. The difference was very sharp and clear in my case studies. The change can be observed for families that move from one kind of setting to the other. The change can be *felt* when one makes such a transition oneself. In the unmodernized situation, family members are drawn into collective work. In the modern home, this effort tends to go slack.

• A third possible answer to the question is: We do not really know how strong the correlation is, between modernization in the home and laziness of the children. There are exceptions. I think it is a strong correlation, but I could be wrong. A large, elaborate, controlled study has yet to be done.

Figure 1 represents the correlation. Most cases fall (I think)

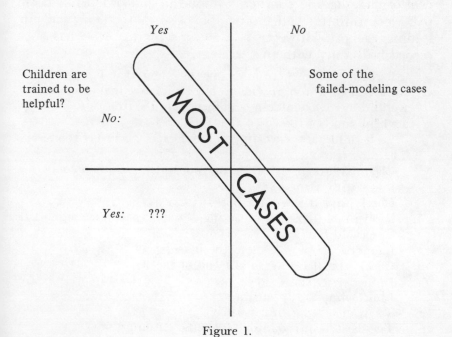

Figure 1.

in the two diagonal cells; unmodernized homes with helpful children and modernized homes with unhelpful children. The other two cells represent the exceptions: "failed-modeling" homes, where children were exposed to serious work socialization, but it did not "take"; and modernized homes that still produce helpful children. This last cell, the bottom lefthand one, would be the most useful one to understand. What did these parents do to reverse the trend?

The general direction of the answer is to be found in the next chapter, I think, and in the advice of authors such as Krumboltz and Spock. The child's willingness can be kept alive, if the parent is skillful enough.

One thing a parent can do is to artificially increase the work that "needs" to be done, by acquiring a pet, making a garden, or raising standards of household neatness and cleanliness. This is a solution that demands considerable effort and determination from the mother. The outcome can be simply a great deal of nagging and conflict, without an end product of positive work training and motivation. The mother may end up feeding the pet. However I know one mother who has succeeded brilliantly with this strategy.

> Barbara took exception to my statement that life-giving work is needed to train kids to be helpers. She manufactures work for her two children, and then takes the trouble to keep at them and bear down so that they do it.
>
> Each child has a checklist on the door of his or her room. The nine-year-old girl's list read like this:
>
> Clean bathroom, MWF (scrub tub, toilet, sink, and counters with cleanser)
> Check Mike (the guinea pig) twice a day
> Dinner table (clearing or setting, she rotates with her eight-year-old brother)
> Laundry, MFW (take it to the basement)
> Check yard (for toys, at the end of the day)
> Dinner time (show up
> Lunch time   on time)
> Teeth, hair (three times a day)
> Tuesday: clean room for Mary (the cleaning lady)

Your room: tidy it, and weed the closets. Put clean laundry away. [The little girl's room was immaculate and in perfect order, down to the contents of her closet and her dresser drawers.]

Barbara says she adds extra chores in the summertime and lightens the load somewhat during the school year. As they get older, she searches for newer and more demanding chores for them, taking pains not to assign them jobs that are too difficult and too grown-up.

The children seem very responsible and very attuned to the niceties of household maintenance. Their workload seems rather light, in terms of time spent on the chores or arduousness of the work. But there are a good many things they must remember to do every day.

PAYOFFS FROM FAMILY HELPING

Why make the effort to try to train the children to be helpers? If you do not, says Dr. Spock, you are apt to produce children "who are self-centered, demanding... It develops adults who in their jobs and in their marriages expect to be pleased and favored. They have little awareness of what needs doing, whether on a picnic or in the office.... Every teacher in nursery school and elementary school has learned that children will develop an increasing sense of responsibility from helping her and the class; and they won't if they don't."[5] In other words, helping makes the child more helpful, considerate, unselfish, and responsible. Nonhelping has the opposite effect. This is the general hypothesis. Its support comes from the Whitings' research, from my own case studies, and from observations by other persons such as Dr. Spock. At best, the hypothesis must be oversimple. For one thing, different households present different kinds of work situations; mothers have different styles. Barbara's army top-sergeant approach seems to foster "responsibility," in the sense of remembering to do this-and-that. Having little brothers and sisters to care for

---

[5]Spock, *Problems of Parents*, pp. 46-47.

might tend to emphasize "altruism": nurturing the little ones, having forebearance, and letting their needs come before yours. A farm might be more apt to produce "hard workers," kids who were hardened to very arduous work and even did it willingly. The resulting motivation and need disposition in the child might have all sorts of colorations and shadings of feeling, depending on what was emphasized in the household work situation.

The helpful children — those who are trained in childhood to be helpers — presumably grow into helpful and responsible teenagers. And they go on to become adults who help out and are good sports in their own homes. This is another open question, of course — how much any effects of helping, in childhood, persist in later life. My case studies suggest that early helping provides a foundation, which then can be built upon a variety of ways, depending on what line of development a young person takes. Different kinds of teenage careers and adaptive styles appear to get their start in early household work. Altruistic, child-care-oriented girls; girls who develop a "cope-by-organizing" style; and precocious teenagers, who impress grown-ups as being very responsible and therefore get opportunities to do grown-up things — these are three such lines of development. Certain superior work habits, and mechanically based hobby careers, can also be traced (in some cases) to early work in the home.

Helping in the home, children also learn useful skills. Cooking is a good example. If you live alone at some time in your life, you will have to prepare your own meals. When you marry, you will no doubt be called on to cook and work in the kitchen. If you do the job well (and willingly), this will have a bearing on the quality of your life (and your family's). For economy and health reasons, as well as life enjoyment, how well the cook does her job is important.

So an added reason for early work-training, in the home, is learning useful skills: learning to cook, learning other housework skills and child care, learning to do certain mechanical repairs. More important than learning to cook eggs or to fix a faucet leak is getting off to a good start in these areas of work, so that you can learn more, and get good at them, as you grow into adulthood. Getting off to a good start has to do, again, with the problem of instilling positive motivation. It will be a recurring theme throughout the next two chapters.

One more hypothesis: Children never learn appreciation until they have done some of the work themselves.

We tell our five-year-old to say thank you; we remind him when he forgets. His perfunctory "thank you's" do not really express gratitude. He has no awareness of what is involved in fixing him a dessert, or buying him a present, or doing any of the things that we do for him. These same perfunctory "thank you's" I have heard from older children, from teenagers, who had never been taught to do the work in the house.

Other children, who have crossed over to join the team of responsible people who run the home and do the work, have more appreciation of what lies behind the meals and all the rest. I would guess that they even "appreciate" their parents more, in the sense of seeing the parents' side of things. They certainly "appreciate" in the sense of having more awareness of what the parents do for the family. The appreciation comes from working alongside the parents on common tasks.

Part II
How Children's Work Styles Develop

Chapter 8

ENCOURAGING HELPFULNESS

THIS chapter tries to explain what is meant by good parental handling, good teaching and bad, skillful parents, mistakes, abuses, botching the job. The answers come mainly from two source books: *Problems of Parents* by Dr. Benjamin Spock, and *Changing Children's Behavior* by John and Helen Krumboltz. The answers may not seem like sensational revelations; but they are, in effect, the tip of an iceberg. Behind the Krumboltzes' book lies the entire behavior-modification approach; and it is, I think, a powerful one for explaining and shaping behavior of this sort. The behaviorist approach (as represented by the Krumboltz book) is very briefly presented in this chapter. I return to it in the next chapter, *Encouraging Interests and Aptitudes*.

I also raise issues that are suggested by my cases: how helpfulness develops, stages that are passed through; children who change from "lazy" to helpful; and how a conducive home situation (need for the child's help) can overcome parents' mistakes.

"HELPING" AT AGE THREE

When little children first try to assist their mothers, they are too young to be of any help. Their efforts to participate in her housework are merely a bother. A mother may, gently or roughly, shunt the child aside; or if she is truly heroic, she can try to give the child a sense of inclusion in her work.

[When I'm working in the kitchen and she wants to help, I try to find some way to include her.]
"What's that you're doing?"
"I'm putting in sugar. See? Taste it." [On the finger . . . and so on through the steps of her cooking until the

child loses interest and wanders away.]

> Valerie, aged two and one-half, wants to help with the baking of bread. Her mother dips the cup into the flour [Valerie could not do that yet without making a mess of it], then hands the cup to Valerie, who pours it into the mixing bowl.

> Working in the kitchen, Joy asks her mother where the potatoes come from. The mother begins a serious explanation, reminding Joy of last summer when they worked in the garden. The child's interest soon wanders.

Letting a three-year-old "help" requires the same kind of special effort as does answering the child's questions in a serious fashion. It is easier to ignore or discourage her overtures or distract her with something else to do. Only conscientious and hardworking mothers with considerable resources of imagination are able to this. Even they will lapse into discouraging responses at times, when the barrage of demands and questions has worn down their patience. If fresh reinforcements can be brought in — an older girl, the father, or a grandmother — the child may get more good teaching of this sort.

Is all this sacrifice worth the effort? When children are a little older, they can actually do small tasks; they can be given instructions and they are less intrusive and demanding. Assisting, they are much less bother; they can even provide some real help. Why go to all this trouble at age three?

We do not know, of course, if it is worth it or not. It is an admirable style of mothering, a touching sight to behold. Some of the young people in my sample who seem to be willing workers and helpers appear to have had mothers who did this. Each of us, when we were at this stage of life, must have emitted x number of questions and offers of help, and we must have received a certain number of ignoring-rejecting responses and some inclusion responses. If the proportion of inclusion responses was favorable, our questions and efforts to become involved must have been encouraged. One would imagine that this would provide a foundation of positive motivation for household work, and a positive attitude toward asking questions, asking to be included, and offering to help.

When a mother gets tired of her three-year-old's "help," if she tactfully diverts his attention and distracts him with something else, this may be a fairly harmless alternative. It is ignoring-rejecting that is neutral, rather than negative and angry, in tone. It is a way of lightening her load.

FROM "HELPING" TO REALLY WORKING

"Children contain within themselves the seeds of all the motives that are needed for cooperativeness. The seeds are sprouting well by two and three years. The hard job for the parents is to cultivate them patiently for the following fifteen years."[1]

If little children start out eager to help, why are older children not similarly eager?

Part of the answer is that "helping" becomes more arduous when the child is older. The demands are greater, and the quality of his work motivation must be different. A three-year-old's eagerness to participate and be included is different from the acquired work motivation that older persons may develop: for example, Virginia's satisfaction in being the accountable, responsible member of the family (*Child Care* chapter); a farm boy's pride in being a hard worker, even at very arduous and monotonous work; a teenager's need for grown-up competence and for recognition that he is competent; maternal "instinct"; and interest in child care, cooking, mechanical problem solving, and in other kinds of work.

When Michael asks to "help" at some task such as setting the table and is actually given a job to do (such as putting out the napkins), his task performance is spotty at best. What he really wants to do is to participate, not to work. Work, by definition, must be done on its own terms. A job has its own particular requirements. To do the job properly you must conform to the requirements, rather than express your spontaneous desires. (Mark Twain said, "Work consists of whatever a body is obliged to do. . . . Play consists of whatever a body is not obliged to do.") Real work tends to become repetitive, boring, con-

---

[1] Benjamin Spock, *Problems of Parents* (New York, Fawcett World Library, 1962), p. 50.

fining, or frustrating and difficult. The small child's tendency is to pursue his spontaneous inclinations and not follow the task to completion; and he may not pay enough attention to instructions to do the job properly.

My wife disagrees. She thinks children really want to do the work — even arduous work — if they can *work alongside the parent*. As long as working means being included, their interest does not waver. Perhaps the truth lies somewhere between our two views.

At any rate, as the child gets older, age three, four, five, six . . . mere participation changes to doing actual chores. Gradually, perhaps, a critical step is taken: from playing at working, to actually working. When the stern requirements of the job at hand take over, then surely it must be harder to sustain positive motivation.

Perhaps a lot of the trouble begins at this critical juncture.

WORK CAN BE PLEASANT OR UNPLEASANT, INTERESTING OR BORING, DEPENDING ON HOW IT IS MANAGED

"The real meat of the discussion is: What makes children unwilling or willing to be helpful around the house? The largest factor in a child's balkiness is his feeling that the job is basically unpleasant and oppressive. This feeling usually does not come from the nature of the chore itself; since under different circumstances he may be positively enthusiastic about doing the same thing (when visiting another family, for instance!)"[2]

What would Dr. Spock advise to motivate a child to work? Work alongside him, and approach the work in a positive fashion.

In most cases the cause is the tone of voice of the parent when assigning the job or giving a reminder. Goodness knows there will be plenty of reasons why a mother will be irritable when asking her daughter to stop her play and clean up. There's a mess and perhaps some damage. There may

[2]Ibid., pp. 48-49.

have been a lot of squabbling between the kids all afternoon, or there's too little time before supper, or it may be simply that the car or television set has broken down again. But most often it seems that we parents easily fall into a killjoy tone when assigning a duty. If I'm right about this, I think it's an attitude left over from our own childhoods. One of the commonest and most frustrating aspects of human nature is that what our parents did to us in childhood that made us cross we have a way of doing to our own children in turn — even though we disapprove of it. If we resented the way our chores were assigned us in childhood, that irritable feeling is apt to creep into our directions to our children.

But there are more cheerful aspects to all of this. The first is, though it's hard to remember, that children want — more than anything else — to be grown up and do the grown-up thing, especially the things that their parents do. They not only want to do the glamorous things like drive cars and have babies, they want to do housework and mend the plumbing. You can hardly keep a two-year-old from sweeping, or a three-year-old from making a cake when you do. A father has to push his own son away from the workbench when it's necessary for safety or efficiency.

Futhermore, children positively love to be helpful if their efforts have generally been appreciated. They feel particularly proud of themselves when they take the initiative in doing a job. Another favorable factor is that children, like adults, get tremendous satisfaction from bringing the job itself to completion — the joy of workmanship.

One problem we have to keep in mind is the discrepancy between the motives of a parent and of a child in regard to household jobs. Having the lawn look good, the house clean, the dishes promptly washed and put away are distinctly adult concerns, because adults like orderliness, want to make a respectable impression on neighbors and visitors and have pride in their home. None of these means a thing to children. They like to set tables, do dishes, wash cars because they want to be like and want to help their parents. (By ten or twelve the need of money becomes powerful too.)

Therefore, to keep them at such duties parents not only have to be reasonably agreeable about them, but should try to continue to perform them alongside their children as much as possible. You may be able to turn such duties over to children as they get older and more responsible, but if you try it too soon most of the enthusiasm goes out of the occupation. Of course even for grownups such chores will be not only less boring but positively enjoyable when done in company. Even a two or three-year-old will have fun putting toys away if the mother is doing it too, and making a game of it. And dishwashing in some families is the most harmonious time of the day.[3]

Dr. Spock discusses other issues: setting an example for the child; choosing tasks that are appropriate to his age, knowing what he should be able to do, and what is too much to expect; and the effect of pay on the child's willingness to work. But his main points are the above two: participative work and the positive approach. These recur in other writings on this subject.[4]

What does a positive approach entail?

• It means giving praise, thanks, recognition for the child's contributions; not just taking them for granted.

• Building pleasure into the work: This is a talent that only some mothers (and other work masters) possess. With imagination, some jobs can be turned into a sort of game and given the qualities of play. This is much more likely to happen when the child is working alongside the mother (or daddy, or older sister, or whomever), rather than working alone.

• Finally, a positive approach includes minimizing the negative. Nagging, scolding, doing it in anger, "don'ting" — this may be unavoidable at times, but it detracts from the positive approach. It diminishes the child's liking for the work.

Another factor that is mentioned in the literature, in addition to participative work, and the positive approach, is modeling, the example set by other family members. Krumboltz and Krumboltz, for example, explain altruism as developing out of

---

[3]Ibid., pp. 49-50.
[4]John D. Krumboltz and Helen B. Krumboltz, *Changing Children's Behavior* (Englewood Cliffs, New Jersey, Prentice-Hall, 1972.)

Beatrice B. Whiting and John W. M. Whiting, *Children of Six Cultures: A Psycho-Cultural Analysis* (Cambridge, Harvard University Press, 1975), p. 106.

the example set by the mother plus praise for generous, helping, unselfish acts by the child.[5] The importance of example and modeling within the family is one reason why it is harder to train children to be helpers in modernized, nonfarm homes without a lot of work. Dr. Spock would say: Even in such a household, the example set by older brothers and sisters and by others, when their help is needed, influences the child.

These principles (participation, the positive approach, and setting a good example) must be especially important in the early years, in getting the child off to a good start. But they should continue to operate at all ages. Applying them to the people in my own sample, they make sense out of some cases; but they leave me with an unsatisfied feeling when trying to explain others. For one thing, children change. Especially around adolescence, there are dramatic turnabouts: from helper to nonhelper, and vice versa.

These turnabouts are usually mysterious. Krumboltz and Krumboltz try to explain a few cases like this by applying learning-theory principles. For positive changes — from lazy and disaffected to hard-working and helpful — it may be that a *crucial idea,* something resembling an ambition, has crystallized and then made all the difference. This in turn may result from one critical incident.

> At the age of twelve, Ray could hardly be moved from the television set. He procrastinated about doing his chores because he would rather watch almost any television program. One Saturday afternoon his mother finally persuaded Ray to go out to help his father repair some fences on the ranch. His father was a man of few words and said nothing directly to Ray about his work.
>
> That evening a family friend dropped by and Ray's father mentioned the work his son had done in the afternoon: "Ray worked like a real man." The boy overheard the remark.
>
> After that Ray began to be more cooperative in doing his chores. His father remained as taciturn as ever, but the two of them seemed to work together as a team.[6]

---

[5]Krumboltz and Krumboltz, *Changing Children's Behavior*, p. 234.
[6]Ibid., p. 177.

This can be explained as the delayed effect of praise from an habitual nonpraiser. But it also sounds like an example of an energizing idea: a goal or ambition, to be a "real man" or be recognized as a "real man," suddenly becoming realizable, and therefore motivating behavior.

At any rate, there is still considerable room for mystery, even when individual cases have been partly "explained" by reference to praising, example, participative work, positive approach versus nagging and "don'ting." Also, if the conditions are right for training a child to be a worker, then it seems that the parent can commit a good many atrocities and still get good results. In the *Mechanical* chapter I refer to boys with early mechanical aptitude and interest, whose fathers were also mechanical. Some of these fathers appear to have been terrible teachers. But their example, doing mechanical work, seems to have been more important than their teaching techniques.

Another instance of a good situation overriding bad teaching occurs in farm families and large families, in which children were expected to work very hard and their contributions were taken for granted. (From the parents' point of view: After all, they themselves had known nothing but unstinting labor; they must see nothing special about their children doing the same.) I have some informants who report they worked like slaves and were not praised or thanked. Several express bitterness, but most do not. All, evidently, developed into hard workers. Of course, as the case of Ray suggests, praising has its subtleties and its nuances. Praise that is restrained, infrequent, or not stated in a direct and obvious fashion, can still be a motivator; perhaps it might be forgotten or overlooked later on, when the person described her childhood.

A BEHAVIORIST APPROACH

The book *Changing Children's Behavior*, by John and Helen Krumboltz, is one specimen from a body of writings based on behaviorist psychology and learning theory. Behavior-modification psychotherapists, behaviorist family counselors, designers of programmed instruction, and the theoretical writings that guide them, could all be grouped into this family. It offers a more powerful way of dealing with our problem — how to encourage helpfulness — than do the words of wisdom from Dr. Spock or my gleanings from my case studies. It is probably harder for the layman to understand, keep in mind, and apply in his or her own family than is Dr. Spock. But then any self-help advice is difficult to use. Changing children's behavior generally means changing one's own, and this is probably too much to ask of most parents on a sustained basis. (A behaviorist family counselor could help in putting the advice into action.)

Changing Children's Behavior goes into detail on the subject of just what is entailed in being a good teacher versus a bad teacher. Here are the titles of some of their case study illustrations:

"Picking up toys." (p. 17. The parent searches through a series of possible rewards for tidying up, until she finds one that works.)

"Making one's own bed." (p. 37)

"Neglecting to set the table." (p. 46. Why it is important that a parent take the time to get her child to do an assigned chore. It is easier and quicker to do the chore yourself. But then you reinforce the child for *not* doing it.)

"Remembering to feed the pets." (p. 79. Reminding the child to do a chore — termed *cueing*. Ideas for automatic cues are suggested that avoid nagging and negative-toned reminders.)

"Watering the lawn." (p. 81)

"Cooperating in family chores." (p. 81)

"Enjoying increased responsibility." (p. 113. A skillful father, working alongside his son, makes the boy so eager to do yard work that he would rather cut the grass than play with his friends.)

"Learning to take initiative." (p. 130)

"Helping to keep windows clean." (p. 174)

"Increasing willingness to do chores." (p. 177)

————

Dr. Spock's recommendations appear here, phrased in the

language of learning theory. Working alongside the child, and praise, are positive reinforcers. Nagging, anger, and conflict built into the chores represent negative reinforcers. Very much of this, and the child won't want to do it. Failure, especially during the early learning of a task, is also a negative reinforcer. In other words (Dr. Spock's point), make the chore appropriate to the child's age; don't give him a too-grown-up, too-difficult job. Modeling is discussed too, in learning-theory terms.

If you want to shape the child's behavior in a particular fashion (to produce willingness and competence at some household chore), you start out by analyzing the situation (setting the table or whatever), and you ask, What could serve as a positive reinforcer? Some possible rewards might be success at the early trials (doing it right), recognition and praise, working alongside mother, and being graduated up to more grown-up tasks. You try out various reinforcers and stay with any that seem to work. (In some situations, it is not so easy to divine just what might reinforce the behavior that you want to encourage.) If the job is fairly complex and difficult — especially if the child is having trouble with it — you can break it down into its component parts and work on these separately. In situations where the difficulty of the tasks can be controlled and "dosed," a variety of reinforcement schedules can be tried. Following the approach of the programmed-instruction designers, one can sometimes arrange a series of tasks that are so easy, and which get harder so gradually, that the child always does them right — and is rewarded (presumably) by his own success. Or (perhaps after some early successes) the difficulty can be increased more steeply, so that the challenge is greater and doing it right is aperiodic rather than constant.

This way of thinking offers both a detailed guide — for starting a child out right in some area of behavior, and for trying to turn him around, if he has gotten off to a bad start — and it also offers a fund of explanations for particular successes and failures. Needless to say, like all explanations they are hypothetical and not the last word. But their cumulative impact is strong. It is an apt language — I think — for talking about good teaching and bad. It says, for one thing: Loving

care and good intentions are not enough; if you are not skillful
you will botch the job. This raises the question: How did
uninformed humankind, throughout the ages, do as well as it
did? How did *any* children develop into willing workers?

Part of the answer must be: the behaviorist principles overlap
traditional commonsense practices. Part of the answer: A conducive situation makes up for parents' mistakes, especially
where the child's help is genuinely needed, and where there is
cultural support for helpfulness (as with the primitive villages).
Part of the answer is: Even these explanations fall short; how
children become motivated is still somewhat mysterious.

Chapter 9

ENCOURAGING INTERESTS
AND APTITUDES

THIS chapter has to do with getting children off to a good start in various types of work, so that they like the work and do it reasonably well. Work takes place in different arenas: school, home, farms, workshops, and various places of employment. There are myriad kinds of work. In school, for example, there is reading and writing, and the subjects that are based on it (English, history, and social studies, etc.); and there is mathematics and the scientific subjects that flow from it. Within the separate subjects there are subdivisions (within biology, botany, ornithology, and so on). Even these break down into various tasks, skills, and specialties. Within mechanical work, there is woodworking, metalworking, small-appliance repair, watches, photography, electronics, automotive work, and the skills and specialties within these. And there are different kinds of housework, various chores associated with baby care, innumerable things the farmer and the farm wife have to do, and so forth.

As an individual develops, his own pattern of liking and aptitude unfolds. He takes to some activities and not to others. This can have the appearance of God-given talents and in-born incapacities: being able to sing a major triad but unable to roller skate, being gifted at piano but unable to hit a curve ball. Innate endowment must play some part, but I assume that the more complex and judgmental activities — such as reading and cooking and doing housework — are largely the product of learning. This would include just about everything under the aegis of *work*. Although innate talents may make it easier for some persons to do some things, this can be helped along (by good teaching) or thwarted (by bad teaching). I also assume that there is a strong positive correlation between interest and aptitude. We like what we are good at, dislike what we are bad at. Being good at something makes you like it. And being interested in something makes you practice it, so that you get good at it.

Some tasks are intrinsically rather grubby and monotonous. Housecleaning and weeding are examples. Making allowance for this, most chores and work situations can be pleasant or unpleasant, interesting or deadening, depending on how they are managed. Even the monotonous jobs can be lightened if the people sing together while they work (as with African work songs or slave songs) or if people enliven the work in other ways. As a boy, I worked in my grandmother's garden, and in the yard of another lady. Working for my grandmother was a delight, for the other woman it was drudgery. Positive motivation versus negative motivation: it depended simply on a difference in approach.

In general, I concur with Dr. Spock: Aversions for the ordinary kinds of work must be acquired, they are not innate.

To summarize the assumptions:

Aptitudes (and ineptitudes) are largely learned.

So are interests and aversions, likes and dislikes for particular kinds of work.

Liking and aptitude (for some activity) go together. It is all-of-a-piece.

This chapter overlaps chapter 8, *Encouraging Helpfulness*. The same points apply to both. To maximize liking for some task or at least minimize dislike:

• It is better to work alongside the child. Participation, togetherness, and a sense of joint effort is reinforcing. (Exception: this must not be true in cases where parent and child [or older brother and younger brother, or whatever the work group is] cannot work together without a great deal of conflict.)

• Accentuate the positive. Recognition, thanks, and praise are reinforcing. Doing it in anger, nags, and "don'ts" are aversive.

Presumably, if early experiences with some type of work are positive, then a liking for this work is more apt to develop, so that participative work, a positive approach, and anything that can make the work rewarding is particularly important when the child is just beginning. Krumboltz and Krumboltz have a number of things to say about getting children off to a good start in some area of work: noticing and recognizing early efforts; rewarding first attempts; and arranging for early successes.

Some of the literature on learning bears on these subjects: within educational psychology (learning in school situations), and the more abstract, high-level treatments of learning within academic psychology. Perhaps what follows will be a bit oversimplified. My wish is to discuss this clearly and to stay close to the practical question: What can we do with our children, to help them have a positive approach to work?

GETTING OFF TO A GOOD START

The Krumboltzes are not just concerned with helpfulness, of course, but with the more general subject of how to shape children's behavior in a desirable direction. Some of their case examples have to do with interests and aptitudes:[1]

"Generating enthusiasm for school." (p. 5. Interest versus boredom. One problem with school is that, since it is taught to groups, the teacher cannot make individualized reinforcement schedules.)
"Motivating a vocal music class." (p. 12. Searching through a series of possible reinforcers to find one that will work.)
"Learning to enjoy reading." (p. 14)
"Developing independent study skills." (p. 31. Breaking down a complex activity into component tasks and skills and working on these one-by-one.)
"Learning to cook." (p. 121)
"Learning to care for plants." (p. 168)

When children are learning something new, they can be discouraged by early failures. So you let them succeed every time at first, if this can be arranged. You do not give them a job that is too much for them. As they succeed at early trials and get

[1] John D. Krumboltz and Helen B. Krumboltz, *Changing Children's Behavior* (Englewood Cliffs, New Jersey, Prentice-Hall, 1972).

better, you can then step up the demands and make the task harder. But first there should be only positive reinforcers. Their two examples are a father teaching his little boy to play chess — first the child gets to "win" every game, then gradually the father plays better and wins some games himself — and a little girl learning to cook (first easy successes and later harder jobs with some failures).[2]

Presumably, a person's pattern of likes and dislikes and talents develops on this kind of foundation. Little children are exposed to basic areas of functioning — mechanical manipulations, writing with a pencil, reading — and to derivative work situations (using a screwdriver, wielding an axe, school). Some get off on the right foot, perhaps accidentally and unnoticed. Others do not. Some activities are congenial and others uncongenial, as a result of early successes and failures. Your personal inclinations toward certain kinds of work are based on early success experiences.

"I loved woodworking, from my first manual training course. I loved the way the wood smelled. I took to it. Metal shop was different. I couldn't get the solder to melt. Some kids seemed to do it easily. I didn't. And I've never liked to work with metal or machinery. It makes me sick."

Off to a good start, a child will presumably practice and get better. Off to a bad start, after a few failures he will dislike and, hence, avoid that kind of work. An example, used at the beginning of the *Failed Modeling* chapter, is learning to read. Whether reading comes easily or hard, quickly or slowly, pleasurably or painfully can determine a child's chances for success in school (so the argument goes). By third grade, some children will have read perhaps ten times the material that others have read; they will be able to read much more advanced material, and read it more easily, read faster, and get much more out of their reading. Not only are they better able to learn and enjoy themselves via reading, but they will probably do well in their other school subjects and be typed as good students. Any child who gets bogged down in the beginning is in grave danger of

---

[2]Ibid., pp. 117-123.

falling behind, having humiliating experiences in school, and as a result disliking school and never doing well.

VARIOUS INSTIGATORS OF INTEREST

The teacher's role in instilling interests is then twofold. (By "teacher," I mean the parent or whoever introduces a child to some kind of work.) First of all, the teacher creates the situation and arranges for the child's first successes. She "makes it happen." Usually the child cannot do this by himself. Second, the teacher can serve as a role model. A little girl understudying her mother, learning housework and child care, is doubly motivated — if the mother does her job well. The mother arranges a series of pleasurable learning experiences, full of little successes, which encourage the girl in her work. And the little girl emulates her mother and wants to be like her. The result in each case is positive motivation, interest in child care, even in housework. Ambition to be like the mother and do what mother does must combine with pleasurable and successful experiences, to produce a lasting interest in child care and homemaking. The same would be true for other success cases of mechanical fathers and sons, farmers and their sons, and so on.

Older children may become fired with ambition in some line of activity because a teacher comes along and gets them interested. (If they haven't already been ruined in this area by bad experiences).

Robbie enrolled in tenth grade biology with the same perfunctory spirit with which he enrolled in any course. It was merely to fulfill a requirement.

The biology teacher, Mr. Barnett, was a favorite among many of the students in Robbie's class, especially the boys. He would occasionally plan short field trips during laboratory periods. At the request of some of the students he also devoted some of his Saturday mornings to taking longer field trips with students who volunteered. They would look for specimens of plants and insects, observe their characteristics carefully, write down their observations, and classify their findings. Mr. Barnett asked many questions and encouraged his students to ask questions also. He was never satisfied with mere opinions. He insisted that the students answer questions from their own direct observations or the observations of the scientists who wrote the biological reference books.

Robbie became an avid information seeker. He spent much of his free time on hikes looking for insects for his new collection. He kept a notebook on his "research work" and shared his findings enthusiastically with his classmates and his family.[3]

Among my cases are people whose career goals were determined, they say, by someone in their childhood.

Jill, a physical education student at Dalhousie University, a competitive swimmer and a swimming teacher in the summertime, traces it all to a Red Cross swimming instructor she had when she was a little girl. This woman made a strong impression on her and got her interested in serious swimming. Her admiration for her teacher seems definitely to have influenced her ambitions. She has worked hard at her swimming; to be a swimming instructor is her career choice.

Susan shows a straight-line development in her emulation of her mother; from helping her mother in the home, caring for her younger siblings, and doing housework; to being a candy striper in the hospital in which her mother was a nurse; to entering nursing school herself.

In other cases, something happens to unleash a teenager's motivation. The two Krumboltz examples illustrate this: Robbie, who became interested in field biology; and the earlier example of Ray, who suddenly became fired with ambition, working for his father. A pent-up need for grown-up competence, and a need to be recognized as having grown-up competence, is supposed to be very strong in teenagers.[4] When the right idea or ambition comes along — so that the youth "sees" how this recognition might be achieved — he may suddenly start working feverishly. Wanting to be like a role model — or seeking recognition from a role model — plays a large part in these ambitions, I think. The ambitions must often be ill-

---

[3]Ibid., p. 62.

[4]Erik H. Erikson, "Identity and the Life Cycle," *Psychological Issues*, *1*:1959.

Erik H. Erikson, "Youth: Fidelity and Diversity," *Daedalus*, *91*:5-27, 1962.

Robert J. Havighurst, *Developmental Tasks and Education* (New York, David McKay Co., 1972).

founded, short-lived, fantasy, doomed to disappointment. But cases like this, sudden fits of ambition, must blend into other cases such as Susan and Jill, who have maintained their general direction over a period of years. Someone should study this phenomenon, and follow some of these young people over a period of years. A hypothesis: Who the role model is has much to do with the practicality of the youth's ambition. A responsible adult, with whom he works, is more apt to inspire a workable ambition than is a teenage idol or an admired adult who is not known personally.

Superficially similar to teenagers' spurts of interest, which are based (I think) on ambitions, is the phenomenon of *readiness*. When children's exposures to things to learn are not regimented by school study plans, the children spontaneously elect to learn geometry, skating, appreciation of classical music, use of a sewing machine, interest in adventure novels, and so on, at times of their own choosing. When a child is ripe for one of these things, he is interested and optimally able to learn it fast and well. Therefore — so this theory goes — the best way to teach children is to give them tentative exposures, and when the child responds to something with interest, go ahead and teach it. Social influence — what their friends are doing, admiration of a role model — must affect how their interests emerge as they get older; but this combines with other mysterious influences, including perhaps a maturational unfolding.*

To summarize the various instigators of interest and hard work that I have mentioned: They include getting off to a good start as a result of early successes; emulating the teacher; an ambition for grown-up competence which includes wanting to be like a role model; and periods of readiness, which possibly have a maturational foundation. The cases suggest a few more instigators. You can ask, *just what does it take, to make someone get down to work?* One girl in my sample will only work hard in school if she likes her teacher. Most of her classes are beneath her contempt, and she does the bare minimum in them. But usually she has one teacher whom she really

---

*The author wishes to thank John Hirshout, Research Computer Systems, New York, New York.

approves of and admires, and for that teacher she gives her all. So her own personal requirement seems to be: She has to be making the effort *for* someone, she cannot just be doing it for herself. If the relationship with her mentor is not to her liking, then she won't work.

A more common requirement, for students and for many people with a job of writing to do, is deadline pressure. They cannot get down to work until the night before the exam or shortly before the paper is due.

A third requirement is that the job be interesting. In my sample are a number of youths who have had brilliant hobby careers, but they have done poorly at school. They seem too proud, or too "spoiled" by turned-on work, to submit to a dull routine. They are an extreme example of our common tendency to work more willingly when we are interested. One would imagine that they will have to accommodate somewhat to dull routine, in order to get through life.

EARLY EXPOSURES IN BASIC AREAS OF FUNCTIONING

In exposing children to different kinds of work and play, getting them off to a good start is to be desired. But even more important is avoiding a bad start. Don't ruin them. In my sample are several "mechanical" men who say they did not start mechanical work until they were grown-up. For some reason, they never got around to it until some time in adulthood. Then, when they got interested, they learned quickly. They must have been able to do this because they were not ruined as children. Other people are mechanically inept, fumbling, and stupid, and they tend to avoid mechanical work. They must have been ruined, probably in fairly early childhood. If not ruining a child is the first priority, and teaching him well is the second, then theoretically it might be best to avoid some of these important areas for awhile. At an older age, perhaps an individual is not so vulnerable to bad handling. However, in practice it may be nearly impossible to protect a young child from early exposures in basic areas.

For example, manual dexterity seems to be basic to mechanical work. Although one's hands may be skilled in one type of work and fumbling in another — as with the boy who could not get his solder to melt — there is quite likely a general manual dexterity factor. Or, something happens to some people, early in life, so that they are generally bad at working with their hands, using screwdrivers and hammers and needles. Perhaps there is a genetically transmitted handicap; or perhaps the bad example of a fumbling parent is important. At any rate, a little child in his play can be learning his bad manual habits for some time, before he is ever deliberately taught the use of a screwdriver and hammer and nails. Other basic afflictions — clumsiness, shyness — might similarly rest on such an early foundation. Mechanical talent and interest may be based on *positive* learning trials like this, in the first few years of life. Success in reading and writing — basic to school success — seems to be influenced by some sort of word sense, which is already developing in the preschool years.[5]

It is, of course, not known just how early a child becomes a hopeless case in some area of endeavor. There are probably strategic periods of life — varying from one child to the next — for teaching well (or avoiding) particular things. And probably the basic skills (such as manual dexterity), for which learning starts in early childhood, do not play a critical role in learning certain other things (such as growing a garden, caring for a baby, baking bread, or presiding over a meeting). In other words, it is not all decided in early childhood. Later exposures must be important, too, for some interests and aptitudes.

---

[5]Hans Furth and Harry Wachs, *Thinking Goes to School: Piaget's Theory in Practice* (New York, Oxford Press, 1974).

J. F. Cavanaugh and I. G. Mattingly, *Language By Eye and By Ear* (Cambridge, MIT Press, 1972).

Chapter 10

WORK HABITS

THIS chapter has to do with the way work is done. "Lazy," "a hard worker," "ability to follow instructions," "finishes what he begins," "high standards," "disciplined," "a coper," "well organized," and "perseveres when things go wrong" — these terms represent some of the traits that are involved. The discussion will overlap the previous chapter. Behaviorist learning principles and examples from Krumboltz are cited once more; also, learning by example, copying a teacher's work habits.

There are all kinds of variables involved in any consideration of people's work styles. Down on the farm, they talk about one youth who is "a worker" — meaning he is willing and industrious and capable of completing a lot of work — versus another who is "lazy." One youth is a "self-starter." He can, by himself, "see what has to be done, and do it." Another boy has to be told what to do, every step of the way. He cannot, on his own, "see what has to be done next." I, as a child, was characterized as a "plugger," meaning I would work away at a boring task until it was done. A number of large-family girls in my case studies learned to handle their overload of work by becoming very efficient, resorting to lists, and being highly organized; they had a cope-by-organizing work style. Some other dimensions are: planning ahead versus not planning your work realistically; being neat and organized versus disorganized and messy; finishing what you start versus tending to leave it lying there unfinished; perfectionistic, meticulous, high standards; and so on. This is a vast territory which can be mapped and divided up in a variety of ways, depending on the terms and constructs used.

The list of characterizing terms that I have collected can be grouped under two more general master-variables: *discipline* and *coping*. Under *discipline* are such traits as "a willing, hard

117

worker," "finishes what he starts," "orderly," "punctual," "dependable," and how high one's standards are. *Coping* has more to do with intellectual style and capacity: problem-solving ability, handling the more complex jobs of organization (for example, thinking in terms of a flow chart), initiative, alertness.

There must be a strong correlation between work habits and ability. You can start out talking about a person's work habits and find you are evaluating how effective he is. To a great extent, I suppose, the work habits do add up to ability.

If you try to type persons whom you know as "lazy," "well organized," "a self starter," and so on, you run into a number of difficulties. These terms are stereotypes which do not do justice to the fluctuations, variations, unevenness, and contradictions in people's actual behavior. In addition, there are many different kinds of jobs and work situations. A person is probably "lazy" in some, "hardworking" in others; has initiative in some and not in others. As we grow up, go through school and go into the work world, and try out different kinds of work — fixing a car, doing algebra problems, running a meeting, holding an elective office, public speaking, manual labor, and so on — we discover that we can cope well with some of these situations and not with others. You can have good work habits in some areas, and bad work habits in others. In my own case, I was good in school (and in work that derives from schoolwork) and bad in mechanical work. In mechanical work I was definitely not "a plugger;" I wanted to give up immediately when a mechanical problem did not resolve to an easy solution.

Table I represents work habits and kinds of work in a table. Each cell of the table affords a characterization of a person on one work habit variable for one kind of work. For example, "finishes tasks," in schoolwork, office work, housework, mechanical work, managerial work, other kinds of work: yes or no. Or it could be "usually" versus "seldom," or a numerical score on a ten point scale, or whatever. If you try to characterize somebody (such as yourself) on the table, you will probably come to the conclusion that the table is not detailed enough.

Table I

Work Habits	School- work	Office work	House- work	Mechanical work	Managerial work
Discipline					
Finishes tasks	yes/no	yes/no	yes/no	etc.	
Orderly	yes/no				
Prompt	yes/no				
Dependable	etc.				
Hard worker					
High standards					
Coping					
Problem-solving ability	yes/no	yes/no	etc.		
Organizes efficiently	yes/no				
Plans ahead	yes/no				
Initiative	etc.				
Alertness					

There are different kinds of schoolwork (on which performance varies), different housework tasks, and different varieties of orderliness, and so forth.

Do work habits, learned in childhood, tend to continue into later life? My assumption is that they do, *for similar kinds of work.*

> When Ron was a boy, he was lazy and unhelpful around the house. So were his brother and his sister. Their mother did everything for them. However, Ron always did well in school, and from the time of his first paper route he established a pattern of aggressive hard work in his part-time jobs and summer jobs. He was a hustler.
>
> Now Ron is grown up and married. In his own home, he is useless in the kitchen and does practically no work. He watches television, drinks beer, and lounges. In his government career he has had three promotions in the last two years. He seems to be aggressive, hardworking, and very ambitious.

What are the later applications of various kinds of work in childhood?

Helping out in the home must, at the very least, prepare children to be helpers in their own homes when they grow up. Cooking in childhood must prepare for cooking in later life.

Similarly, one would suppose, the work styles learned around the house (neat and orderly, high standards of cleanliness in housecleaning, etc.) would tend to continue into adulthood. However, I would assume the continuity would be strongest for the person's behavior in the home. One might not be neat, clean, and orderly in certain other situations. This assumption, that work styles continue, *for similiar kinds of work,* is probably overly conservative. Brent (described below) was meticulous in his yard work when he was a little boy; he was anything but painstaking in his schoolwork. He grew up to be a generally perfectionistic person, in schoolwork, yard work, housework, farm work, hobbies, mechanical repairs, learning sports; evidently in everything. Probably in some cases a work habit generalizes, is later applied more widely, in other kinds of work. I also know other people who seemed to have changed, reversed themselves, in their work habits in a particular kind of work (as with Brent in school). The assumption might be better stated: The more similar the work situation or type of work, the more likely an early work habit will be applied in it. What might govern whether a work habit generalizes, or carries over into adulthood at all? Beyond frequency and duration of practice, I have no idea.

Early mechanical manipulations must lay the foundation for later mechanical work, coping with repair problems, and the capacity to take up mechanical hobbies. Both ability and work habits for mechanical work must unfold from childhood. As we shall see, boys' mechanical careers show a branching pattern. They progress from working on their bikes to doing household repairs to working on cars, and then they can branch out and follow more esoteric interests. I assume that early learning in an area of work (like the mechanical) then generalizes, provides a foundation, and can be applied when the youth progresses to specialized types of that work.

All of this seems reasonable, but it is without research support. The problem has not been studied. We only have observations and memories of isolated cases. To take an example from another field: Margaret Mead is gifted at noticing bits of behavior by children and comparable or derivative behavior by older people and pointing out the parallel. In Samoa, girls had to stay home and care for babies, but boys ranged the village in play groups. The boys were good at cooperative play. They organized themselves for joint enterprises. For example, a group of little boys would trail after older youths who were going eel hunting on the reef. They would make themselves useful.

> [They] organize themselves into a highly efficient work team; one boy holds the bait, another holds an extra lasso, others poke eagerly about in holes in the reef looking for prey, while still another tucks the captured eels into his *lava-lava*. . . . [For girls] the community provides them with no lessons in co-operation with one another. This is particularly apparent in the activities of young people; the boys organize quickly, the girls waste hours in bickering, innocent of any technique for quick and efficient co-operation.[1]

To return to the question, what are the later applications of work habits learned in childhood:

For schoolwork, the analogous situations in adult life must include working in offices or working with books and records and memos. Various requirements of adult life, such as keeping appointments, being on time, doing your assignment, following written instructions, planning your work and your time so that you meet deadlines, and sitting quietly while someone talks for a very long time — school prepares for these. People who eventually have some success in office jobs, professional careers, and administrative posts presumably did so because (for one thing) they learned fairly good work habits in school, and these later generalized to their jobs.

In addition to work habits, particular skills are learned in school. There are probably core skills for particular kinds of work. They are basic; without mastering them one does not progress very far. Reading is a core skill for school, and for school-derived work situations. Mathematics represents another core skill for the technical fields. Other kinds of work probably have their especially strategic, necessary, core skills.

---

[1]Margaret Mead, *Coming of Age in Samoa* (New York, New American Library, 1949), p. 27.

In addition, there must be critical components to effective functioning in various work situations. In the example of mechanical work which we will be returning to, I think there are two critical elements: some manual dexterity, and a logical problem-solving approach. A third might be added: What do you do when the work hits a snag? Abandon the job, settle for a quick-and-dirty solution, or persevere and do the job right?

I would expect critical components, too, and core skills to show continuity from childhood — in a particular type of work. The case studies of mechanical careers give a little encouragement to this assumption. Manual "knack" for certain kinds of work can be traced from childhood for some cases (as with the boy whose solder would not melt). The other two traits — problem-solving style and perseverence when something goes wrong — are not so easily traced over time. I would assume that they are established in childhood or adolescence, but that they are not necessarily correlated with perseverence in other areas of work or with the way nonmechanical problems are attacked.

HOW WORK HABITS ARE LEARNED

Since the learning of work habits has not been studied (as far as I know), all I can do here is raise some questions. The example set by parents and other role models and teachers of work must be important at times. Neat versus sloppy, meticulous versus careless, punctual versus unpunctual, persevering versus easily discouraged: one would expect traits such as these to be passed along (for a particular type of work), simply in the course of role modeling.

Most of the work habits variables have to do with *standards* — how particular the person is. Does he hold up very high standards for himself? Is he meticulous, a perfectionist? Or is he willing to settle for work which is not so good, less than perfect, flawed, not done in the most thorough way, with less attention to detail? It seems a reasonable hypothesis that parents who have high standards for themselves (in a particular type of work) would try, in teaching their children, to train the children to meet these standards, too. A meticulous house-keeper would train her daughter to be the same way. The same rule would hold for low standards (a sloppy mother allows her daughter to be sloppy, also), and for cases where the teacher of the work is someone else.

On the other hand the correlation may be rather low, be-tween the standards of the mother and daughter; or between farmers and sons; or apprentices to mechanical work and their teachers.

Trying to instill high standards must make the teaching more difficult. At some point — perhaps not with young children but later in the teaching process — the parent would have to become strict, point out small flaws in the work, and insist on an attention to detail which might very well be frus-trating to the child. The potential for thwarting, conflict, and instilling aversion for the work should increase as standards go up.

> Anna is a tomboy. She is one of the few girls in my sample who developed into a lady mechanic. She described for me how she did various mechanical projects, and how meticu-lous she usually was.
>
> I asked her to try to think back to her childhood. How did she become a perfectionistic worker? She said her two little brothers were always razzing her. Any time she did anything, they were there to make comments. If she fixed a lawnmower, they would inspect it and look for something to kid her about. She said her father would also look very carefully at work she had done, and criticize any departures from high standards of workmanship. It was incidents like these that she could remember when I asked her why she developed into a worker with high standards.
>
> But later in our talks, when Anna described how she hated to cook and how she never really learned to prepare meals, she gave the same reason. The family would razz her; she would be the butt of jokes when she cooked something for them. Tomboy that she is, Anna also talked about being razzed for wearing lipstick and feminine clothes.

A fine line — a subtle difference — must divide cases like Anna the noncook (being turned off an activity by too much criticism) from cases like Anna the fine workman (trained to high performance as a result of nit-picking criticism).

How do high standards get instilled without destroying motivation? The gradual shaping of behavior may be the answer in some cases. The parent is patient at first. She is satisfied with low-standard efforts. She rewards and praises work that is in the direction of what she wants. She trys to restrain her own perfectionistic impulses. Can perfectionistic parents restrain themselves like this? I doubt that many can. Perhaps a late introduction to the work, when the child is older, would make the demands (on the parent for patience, and on the child for perfection) less arduous, and increase the chances for success.

Role modeling should also improve the chances for learning high standards. If a little girl is keen to emulate her mother, or a boy wants to be like a mechanic who is teaching him, then *being like* the model might include excelling in the work. Cases of teenagers who are intensely ambitious — to be good at the piano or guitar, or at competitive swimming, or motorcycle technique, or whatever — can be explained in this way. They want to excel. They probably want to be like one or more admired heroes in their field, including (in some cases) their mentor, so they strive for perfection.

Cultural support for high work standards must make this easier than it would otherwise be. In the localities where I have done fieldwork, in the Caribbean and in Spain, standards were extraordinarily low. A child growing up in one of these places, learning by the example of the people he worked under, and conforming to the standards they held out to him, would probably be a very unreliable, careless worker. Of course this generalization would have to be qualified by type of work and by work habit variable involved. At traditional, premodern tasks, where punctuality was no factor, people may have worked well enough. Also, I did come to know a few very superior workers. They were doubly admirable, because they persevered in the absence of the cultural support to be found, for example, in our own society.

According to national stereotypes, two culture areas have very high standards of competence and excellence in work:

East Asia (Japan, China) and Northern Europe (Germany, Holland, Scandinavia). In a high-standards cultural milieu, a youth learning to work would have the example of other people working around him, and he would have generally high standards held up for him. The burden would not simply be on the parent or on the teacher.

To return to our own culture, here is an example of a boy living up to perfectionistic standards. This is Brent, one of the "enterprisers" I will be describing in Chapter 13. In school, he says,

> "I turned the other way. Since I could never hope to do as well as my sister, I wasn't going to try at all. I went out of my way to make things hard on my teachers; I managed to scrape my way from grade to grade. I was labeled an underachiever."

But at home it was different. He describes his chores when he was eight to eleven years old.

> " . . . and keeping the grass cut and flower beds trimmed in the summer, and the long driveway and walks immaculate in the winter months. I would set my alarm clock early in the winter and if it snowed a lot in the night I would clear the driveway so Mom could get to work. My mom and dad were really obsessed with neatness and pride in doing a good job or not doing it at all! After awhile I adopted this attitude and it has had interesting effects upon my various endeavors. I can easily remember cleaning the driveway and walks two times in a day; the driveway and walks weren't just cleared — they were cleaned *right* to the pavement everywhere, with nice straight lines, square corners, and well-shaped snow banks. The lawn was cut in both directions and the cuttings were all raked up; all the edges along the walks and beds were trimmed by hand at a 90-degree angle — it was something else! Although it sometimes took a little nagging to get me going, once I got started I wanted to do a perfect job and I was always proud of my work. This obsession has carried over in many of my later projects, and I'll tell you about it if you're interested."

. . . which he then proceeded to do. At age twenty, he has had an amazing career.

Brent's case points up some of the unanswered questions and

mysteries about work habits. First, there are the apparent contradictions. He describes himself as a strong-minded, independent, "bad" little boy, who terrorized his older sister, was a
semioutcast in his neighborhood, and refused to conform in
school. Yet he conformed to his parents' perfectionistic standards for doing household chores. And he is similarly meticulous today in all his endeavors — even in doing things for fun,
even in school.

Where did Brent's perfectionism come from? How did his
parents instill it in him? They insisted, evidently, that the yard
work be perfect. How did they manage not to teach him to hate
yard work? Were they unusually patient and skillful teachers? I
doubt that very much. Brent's father is like him in certain ways,
including the perfectionism. Somehow or other, his example
must have been passed along. But how? His father was a sales
executive who was away from home much of the time. He must
have spent little time teaching Brent to work and working with
him.

In other cases in my sample, the origins of work habits are
even more mysterious.

> Harry is a very strong, determined, well-organized worker
> — at school, at home, and in his hobbies. His sister is just the
> opposite. His parents are mystified as to how this happened.
> They say he was "always that way." They cannot trace this
> development to anything that they did, or to their own ex-
> ample. The same is true for the divergent development
> of Harry and his sister. It seems to have "just happened" —
> the same parents, the same home training, opposite re-
> sults.

One possible explanation for these mysteries might go
something like this. These stories of how people developed are
merely stories. They are scraps of memory — overgeneralized
and incomplete. With full access to the facts, all these cases
might be explainable by the learning principles in the Krumboltz book. A child's work style is a result of shaping, over a
sequence of learning trials. The shaping probably continues
over a period of years, under several teachers, and no one may
be very aware of what is happening. The sequential learning
could very easily go in different directions for children in the

same family. Something could happen to inspire one child to excel and make another child passively resistant (or "lazy").

Then one might make some allowances for temperamental differences, and for the effects of ambitions and emulating models and that would round out the general explanation.

Returning to the Krumboltz book, various parts of it have some application to this area. Work habits are directly dealt with in two places, which I have mentioned before: the case of Robbie, who acquired scientific curiosity and an information-gathering style from his biology teacher; and the discussion of persistance training. Under the heading *When persistence, patience, and dedication are desired,* they say:

> A dedicated person is one who works for long periods of time without receiving rewards. Why do some people work for days, months, or even years without much reward whereas others give up quickly when things are not going their way? In all probability the different schedules of reinforcement to which they were accidentally exposed influence the extent to which these people persist.
>
> If you want a child to learn to wait patiently, you would reward him at first for waiting only a few seconds. Subsequently you would reward him for waiting a slightly longer interval of time, gradually increasing the interval each time you ask him to wait.[2]

Then they illustrate with a number of examples, including a mother teaching her daughter to cook and a father teaching his little boy to play chess. The father first let his son win, so that the little boy would like the game and not get discouraged. Then the father began to "improve" and won sometimes himself (aperiodic reinforcement).

As an aside on this point: In playing games with my five-year-old I am totally competitive and selfish, so that he loses every time until he gets good enough to beat me. Michael is impossible to discourage. His optimism is unwavering. He always wants to play more. Why does he give the lie to the Krumboltzes' learning principle? His mother thinks he learned a generalized trait of persistence, as an infant, crying to be

---

[2]John D. Krumboltz and Helen B. Krumboltz, *Changing Children's Behavior* (Englewood Cliffs, New Jersey, Prentice-Hall, 1972), p. 121.

picked up: Either that or he was born with it.

The trait of persistence is one determinant of standards. To hold out for high-quality work, one must often persevere in the face of discouragements.

> Angela will work along at a piece of sewing or knitting. When she discovers a mistake, she rips and starts over.
>
> When something goes wrong like this, you can get very disgusted, get angry, get sick of the job, want to quit. Some people are defeated by something going wrong. But not Angela. She never gives any sign that she minds. She just rips and starts over. She goes along until everything is done right.

In doing mechanical work, the critical juncture is the point in a repair job when the work hits a snag. A nut won't come off; or you need a tool that you cannot find or you don't have; or you can't understand the instructions sheet. Some people put down the work at that point, and pick it up again perhaps six months later. Others find a slipshod solution, and get around the obstruction in this way. ("Lose a gas cap, stick a rag in it; lose a dipstick, use a pencil.") Others cannot control their anger. ("My father's solution to a problem is to throw a hammer at it.") The superior worker has the tenacity to persevere when he hits a snag, but persevere carefully, do it right *and* finish it.

HAVING HIGH STANDARDS AND LIKING THE WORK

Standards and motivation are related. Several people commented on this. Anna said liking the job makes you do it better. For her, working on all sorts of jobs, if she has a positive feeling for the work, then she takes pains and is meticulous. But if it is grubby work that she wants to finish and have done with it — then her efforts are perfunctory. She illustrated with the story of a plumbing job she did for a neighbor. Plumbing was a chore for her; she could not get excited about it.

Paul Mills, who was my main theoretician on the subject of enterprise (see Chap. 13), thinks it works the other way, too. Part of his formula for keeping enthusiastic is: lavish attention to detail. He says the quality of a piece of work depends on how much time you spend on it. Be meticulous, spend time getting the little details just right, be proud of what you produce. This (along with several other essential ingredients of work) can keep your interest alive.

The relationship must be circular. People who start out badly in some type of work — they will dislike it or be bored with it; they will do a perfunctory job; and they will not feel pride in their work. Other people may have their interest killed later on, by conditions of employment that do not allow them to do painstaking work. Paul Mills talks about journeyman carpenters and bricklayers and other construction workers, who have to hurry along and cover up mistakes, whose feeling for their work must become debased.

I know some exceptions to this rule that excellence and enthusiasm go together. For example, a workman can be enthusiastic enough, but very sloppy.

> The fishermen in the village of Seal Rocks have what Jay calls "crisis competence." When their boat stops out to sea, they can do something to get it started and get them in safely. Often what they do is unconventional, something a mechanic would say is impossible, like putting milk into the transmission. Jay says they often fix it in such a way that soon there will be another breakdown involving even further damage. The extreme example of short-run fixing is Brendan's father, who fixed a flat tire on Brendan's bicycle by inserting a toothpick in a special way. "It works fine until you hit a big bump."

> This kind of emergency fixing can occasionally save your life when you are adrift at sea; but the men, as a result, have dilapidated equipment and do shoddy work.

> Also, they do not follow printed directions or plans or diagrams when they are installing or building or repairing some piece of equipment. Either they do not read the instructions through, or they don't take the trouble to abide by them. They say, "Oh that's bull, let's try it this way; I think this will work." This trait may come from bad experiences in school. They avoid the printed word. Needless to say, their repair work is ingenious at times, but slipslod.

Making allowance for exceptions like this, I still think there is a broad relationship between high standards and liking, between excellence and motivation.

Getting off to a good start must be critical. You have some early successes, like the work, practice and try hard because you like it, get better, and get more rewards for your good work. If you are trained to have high standards, this can increase your liking. But too much criticism (in the interest of perfection) can turn you off completely. The line must be a fine one. Anna is a case in point.

Part III
New Avenues of Development That Have Opened Up in Modern Society

Chapter 11

MECHANICAL WORK, INTERESTS, HOBBIES

Ever since my brother David was a little boy he has been interested in cars, and he has been taking things apart. Dave's toy cars and trucks usually ended up in pieces. My father, being mechanically minded himself, would allow David under the car with him while he was fixing it, and he also helped Dave make things in the basement with his tools.

For a while Dave ran out of things to take apart, so if you could not find him, all you had to do was look in the attic. There he would be, wrecking Mum's musical jewelry box, taking the alarm clock apart, or destroying some other needed appliance. He was always able to put things back together too, except when he lost parts, which was fairly common.

David also used to sew and make things with me, especially with sticks, clay, and asbestos.

During visits with my relatives in the country, Dave would be in the barn tinkering with tractors and farm equipment. My cousin also owned a garage where David spent a lot of his time during Christmas holidays. This cousin was a drag racer and stock car driver, which really made Dave look up to him.

From the ages of eight to thirteen, Dave was really into making models. After these models were glued together for a week, they would be barely recognizable with new air scoops, breathers, and thrush mufflers fashioned from polyfilla. He would also use the "lost" parts of the appliances to "soup up" his models. He also made (too many to count) go-carts and Soap Box cars, entering them in races and usually winning.

THE possibilities with mechanical work are so vast that boys must specialize. Dave's passion was cars, although the scope of his interests was fairly broad. For other boys the special affinity is for woodworking; strictly mechanical work with machines and appliances is less attractive, although each of my woodworkers has also done a variety of mechanical work. With other boys it is radio-electronics. All sorts of specialties are possible.

Bikes and cars are the most popular. With cars, boys must go through a long fantasy period, working with models, watching, and simulating and rehearsing the real thing. But with bicycles, for-real work can begin at an early age.

"Looking back, I would say that the hobby I embarked on with the most fanaticism was the bike bug. At an early stage of the racer bike craze in the late 1960s, I fell victim. I converted an old three-speed into a modern-style racer. I took that thing completely apart. . . . But soon I wanted better. I invested my life savings of $130 into a new imported French ten-speed. All decked out with a water bottle, rack (fitted with a custom bag I designed and made), pump, toeclips, tool kit, special gloves, and a pair of professional cycling shoes, I would cruise around looking for the steepest hills to climb and the sharpest turns to whip around.

"I thought, talked, and dreamt bikes. I would almost shiver with excitement whenever I entered my favorite bicycle shop. I nearly gave that two-wheeler a name.

"I read bicycle books. I learned the techniques of the pros and learned to adjust a ten-speed with confidence and ease. Friends began seeking help and advice with their bikes. At home I became recognized as the bike expert. Once a year I was put in charge of repair, replacement, and rust removal for the family fleet of bikes.

"Although a motorbike has now replaced my ten-speed, I find that what I learned working on bicycles has spread out into other areas of my life." [That is to say, there was some transfer to other kinds of mechanical work.]

The classic mechanical career begins at about age three — watching, then taking something apart (and probably not getting it back together again). The parents may give the little boy old clocks, motors, or appliances to experiment on. The next stage is work on bicycles, starting at age six or so. From here the careers diverge along their many tracks: cars, hot rods, motorbikes; household repair; appliances; farm-boy mechanics;

electronics and shortwave radio; woodworking and carpentry; science projects; an entrepreneurial career based perhaps on cars or on used parts of some kind; very narrow specialization, such as Volkswagens; and combinations of these. One thing leads to another. Interested, the boy works and learns, meets other devotees, who introduce him to new things and lead him into new interests. The boy's mechanical career is like a grown-up career in these ways:

- It is work oriented.
- The boy makes progress. He learns by tackling new things. He accumulates tools. He makes contacts, friends, buddies. He works his way into the network of youths and adults (in his community) of like interest. He learns the parts stores, catalogues, junkyards, reference books. He learns where he can find advice, help, expertise. (This depends on the resources of the community of course. In a small town he may be fairly isolated.)
- In some sense, the boy must be ambitious. At the very least, he is working to get better. He must have goals: to do various projects, build or acquire various things; and distant dreams — build his own sailboat, or whatever. He must emulate one or more admired older persons in his field — want to be like them, or become as skilled as they are, or acquire what they have.

The father almost always seems to be mechanical himself. He keeps tools, usually fixes things around the house; sometimes he has a workshop. The little boy must begin by watching his father work and wanting to be like him. In some ways it is like a traditional work-apprenticeship in a peasant village or on a farm. But there are differences. It is not necessarily family helping; it is not doing chores. And nearly all these boys go on to work with other people, and emulate (presumably) other models, by the time they reach adolescence.

Some of the fathers of my mechanical boys must have been terrible teachers. Several fathers would not allow a boy to enter their precious workshops. Some made little or no effort to teach their sons. For others, there was so much friction and impatience that the two gave up working together. A number of boys say little about their fathers, but they deny (when asked) that their fathers had anything much to do with getting them into mechanical work. I assume this means an estranged relationship.

These reports are hard to reconcile with my notion of how these interests begin. I would imagine that getting off to a good start is all-important. The child must start out with a few rewarding experiences — taking something apart, manipulating toys, copying his father, or whatever — that fire his interest and motivate him to do more. In this way his interest builds. If he gets recognition and praise, this may help. But success experiences or fun experiences, in and of themselves, may be sufficient. If he gets very much early *dis*couragement, presumably the opposite, negative learning process would unfold; he would grow up *un*mechanical.

How does one explain the boys with bad-teacher fathers? There are several possible explanations.

• The boy got off to his good start very early in life, before his father had a chance to intervene and ruin him. Later, other people furnished teaching and inspiration.

• A conducive situation might overcome the effects of bad teaching. A mechanical father who does some mechanical work around his home can inspire his little boy to follow in his footsteps.

• Poor data, faulty memory: The reality was more complicated, many-sided, changeable, and contradictory than the summing-up that the informant gave me.

• The fathers who sound like bad teachers were doing some good things too. They inspired their sons by their early example. Some of them, at the very least, were available as a resource: for advice, tools, and help when the boy was at an impasse with some project. Beyond this, perhaps they had their good moments as teachers. The particular example I think of is Leslie's father, the Volkswagen mechanic *(see Failed Modeling,* Chap. 6.) He produced one son (Leslie) who was an avid mechanic and another son who was equally turned-off. Working with Leslie, he was simultaneously helpful and belittling. When he came in to help, Leslie seemed to lose his assurance and become awkward. I imagine this father's input was on balance positive for Leslie; the boy seemed keen to follow in his father's footsteps. For the younger brother, the balance (which may be a delicate one) evidently tilted the other way.

• Finally, innate aptitude or some other unsuspected factor may be very important. This is always possible.

These early mechanical careers are unlike adult occupational careers in that they are not done for money. The interest is intrinsic. No commitment, or obligation to family, or monthly paycheck keeps the boy at it. It is by free choice.

To say that the mechanical boys are positively motivated is putting it too mildly. They are enlivened, awakened, energized, challenged, when they are working at it or talking about it. (The opposite state is how I imagine these boys to have been in school much of the time: mind wandering, dull, sleepy sometimes, fidgety sometimes; bored. Some of the most precocious boys did badly in school.)

To a nonmechanical person such as myself, most mechanical work is intrinsically unpleasant. It is a marvel that anyone could be attracted to it. Fine, delicate work can be maddening. Machines and motors are greasy, vibrating, noisome. Outside work and garage work has its hardships. A rusted nut is balky, frustrating, and unaesthetic. But to the enthusiast this evidently does not matter.

The project that he is working at must draw him on, keep him interested. The project can be started, worked on, put down, left unfinished for awhile, come back to, and eventually completed. Mechanical people are often working on several projects simultaneously. There may be an almost-done project, another in a formative stage, a half-finished project abandoned in the basement, a scheme "put on the back burner for awhile." A project must have a certain challenge value. The motivation is inherent in the job, so to speak. The person must visualize a finished project, or a solution to his problem. The idea must energize him. He rises to the challenge.

This is how I imagine a mechanical interest must be like. As for mechanical ability and talent, the three hypothesized critical components, mentioned before, are:

• Manual dexterity: having the knack, the "feel for it"; "your hands know what to do" — versus having "the fumblies," the extreme low point on the dexterity scale. This may be a generalized trait, or it may vary by type of mechanical work.

• Persistence in the face of obstacles; determination to do a job properly.

• Intellectual ability: The crux of it seems to be a basic problem-solving approach. Mechanical people develop coping styles. They have the confidence to tackle a job and try to fix something. Working, they proceed in a logical fashion. They diagnose the trouble by a step-by-step process of elimination. Then they do what has to be done, step-by-step, with some faith that their logical approach will lead to success. When something goes wrong in the work they can persevere, be patient, stay with it.

Nonmechanical people do not seem to have this kind of confidence in the logical approach. When something goes wrong, if first efforts do not avail, they tend to abandon the step-by-step model and regress to superstitious and animistic thinking. "The damned, ornery thing. It won't work;" as if the machine has decided not to work. They are not mechanical copers.

Developing out of the basic problem-solving approach are various kinds and degrees of intellectual ability, flair and insight, knowledge and experience.

MECHANICAL CAREERS

The unfolding of a mechanical career can be viewed in a number of ways. There is the succession of projects; and the series of interests (from bike to go-cart to working on cars); and the development of skills. The mechanical people say: they worked on one thing, then another; in this way they slowly gained confidence; and they accumulated tools, knowledge, and experience that could be applied to new jobs.

Wayne is an all-purpose household fixer. He says,

"I started out as a little boy, taking things apart, trying to understand how they worked, and I tried to put them together again and fix them. I began to realize that I could figure them out. They weren't so complicated. Sometimes they were pretty simple. I got the confidence I could do it. And I got willing to try to fix new things."

Anna is a lady mechanic:

"You build confidence by fooling around, taking something apart — a doorknob that is lying around, or a lock. Maybe when you're bored and don't have anything to do you take apart a clock that won't work. My little brothers were always doing things like that. They took a tractor completely apart, put it back together, and they had a bucket of extra bolts and other little parts left over. It ran better than ever.

"Also, there is something about having to cope with a crisis that really builds your confidence too. Your motor conks out, and you have to fix it to get your boat back to shore. That kind of thing."

Jay did very little mechanical work when he was a boy. His career did not really begin until he moved into a Nova Scotia fishing village. He bought a little house and started remodeling it. The other men helped him, lent him tools, gave him support and advice. Frankie was his main teacher. Jay would watch Frankie tackle a repair job on an unfamiliar machine, reasoning to himself and talking out loud, to demonstrate how simple and logical it was. And Jay proceeded to experiment, take things apart, try to fix them, becoming less fearful that he would make an unredeemable mistake and ruin them. In this way he learned, and got bolder, and he also began to accumulate tools of his own.

"Anybody can learn to do these things if he's got the guts to try. You just go to the junkyard and get a thirty-five dollar automobile, so that nothing much will be lost. And you get the tools. And you get an instruction book. And you do it. After you work for awhile you know how to do it. And you've learned a lot that helps you with fixing other things. You just go on, fixing more things and learning more."

Theoretically, this is how you do it. Actually, perhaps no one is this self-reliant. Everyone needs some help.

Gordon comes the closest to total self-reliance. He is a rarity in a number of ways. He did no mechanical work until he was forty. He spent his life in New York City. He ran a business consulting firm. Then he pulled up stakes, sold his business, bought a Nova Scotia farm, and plunged into the risky enterprise of rural homesteading. Instruction book in hand, with his newly purchased tools, he shored up his barn, built sheds and pens, renovated the farmhouse, and learned how to be a beef cattle farmer.

Gordon's secret is that he was an all-around coper and problem solver. His life in New York had conditioned him in this direction; and this was the nature of his business. Tempered in the competitive furnace of the New York business world, he was tough, strong, and confident that he could move into a new situation and, instruction book in hand, deal with problems he encountered. And he did.

Confidence, "the guts to try"; the nerve to tackle new problems and cope with them, using the logical step-by-step approach — these qualities may grow, in a successful mechanical career. Or occasionally they may be transferred from other kinds of work, as Gordon evidently has done. Several other business entrepreneurs whom I have spoken to talk about operating in this style. It is part of the ideology of engineering.[1] Business schools, teaching by the case study method, give cognizance to logical problem solving. But machinery, which is concrete, complex, and logical in its workings, is a severe testing ground for the step-by-step approach.

HOBBY CAREERS

Some of the branches that a mechanical career can take, aside from bikes, motorbikes, cars and hot rods, appliance repair, household fixing and building, electrical work, radio electronics, science projects, doing things with chemistry sets, wood- and metalworking, and various specialties of the above — like Volkswagens, ham radio, and maintaining farm ma-

---

[1]Howard S. Becker and James S. Carper, "The Development of Identification with an Occupation," *American Journal of Sociology*, *61*:289-298, 1956.

chinery — are in the burgeoning field of crafts: leatherwork, silverwork, and other jewelry-making perhaps combined with being a rock hound; pottery; ceramics; macrame; silk screen; the traditional women's crafts like rug hooking, weaving, dressmaking, and crewel embroidery; and innumerable newly-invented crafts. Tandy Corporation of Fort Worth puts out a large catalogue of crafts, craft materials, and ideas for making new things. (Some of it verges on Jonathan Winters' "knotty pine pillow with a picture of Niagara Falls on it.")

There are other hobbies that require some mechanical ability and coping, if they are to be pursued seriously: photography; camping, fishing, and other woods craft; having a cabin in the woods; sometimes a boy's first car.

Most of us dabble in some of these hobbies. As we grow up we accumulate equipment and books that are relics of abandoned and undeveloped interests: a microscope, long unused, once a gift from Dad; a fine camera and accessories, once purchased at some sacrifice; perhaps a few power tools in the basement; a small firing kiln; a sewing machine; backpacking equipment; a minerals collection, put away in boxes.

This is even more true for children growing up today than it was for their parents. The commercial development of hobby supplies has taken a spurt. Kits and craft supplies, booklets and how-to-do-it courses: the range of offerings is enormous. Every child has to be given Christmas presents and birthday gifts. He will receive some hobby equipment as presents. He will get other exposures to hobbies because his friends are doing it or because he hears about it via the media. A child growing up today will be exposed to many hobbies. He will receive presents, accumulate equipment. He will make a good many starts on hobbies, get many chances.

The actuarial study of hobbies has never been started, as far as I know; but there are some interesting actuarial questions. What hobby would be a good bet for your child? What kinds of hobbies are bad bets? Of all the hobbies he might take up, what would he stand a better chance of staying with for a while, and getting something out of it? What are the various possible benefits (and dangers) in the different kinds of hobbies? What would your child have to do to reap some of the benefits? At the very least, he would have to stay with the hobby for a while and work at it. Involvement — serious and continued involvement — must be a minimal requirement for getting something out of a hobby.

The actuarial question can be asked in a different way. Take any hobby — for example, photography — and all the teenagers and adults who are taking it up at any particular time. Which ones are apt to get seriously involved and have some success? What personal characteristics predict success in the hobby? If the actuarial study were ever made, various background factors would probably emerge: help from the parents, a work place and darkroom at home, decent equipment and training. And personal characteristics too: a past record of persistence at projects and continuous involvement in some other hobby, disciplined work habits in that kind of work.

I would hypothesize — and this could be tested — that mechanical people are much more apt to become seriously involved in these hobbies: to stay with them for awhile, work hard, make progress, and really get something out of them.

Each one of these hobbies is a series of projects to work on: things to make, build, and/or repair. A youth's work history within a particular hobby would be a series of projects. Also a given hobby must have "career" aspects, since the novice learns, works to get better at it, emulates one or more models who *are* good at it, sets goals for himself, has ambitions. The hobbyist's larger career usually includes a number of hobbies. He may pursue several of them simultaneously. His various projects, sitting around the house and in the basement in different stages of incompletion; his scheme put on the back burner; his ideas of what he might like to do next, *Popular Mechanics* articles and ads, plans and diagrams — these represent several interest areas and hobbies. And of course as he gets older his hobbies tend to change. A more comprehensive view of his work history, then, would probably see him progressing along several fronts simultaneously; and it would see one hobby giving away to another at times. To some extent, lessons learned in one line of work must transfer to later ones.

The hobbyist is sustained in his interest by fellow hobbyists. He joins a rock hound club, or a ham radio club, or Ducks

Unlimited. He may take a course. He goes to the Radio Shack®, to the Bicycle Exchange, to Eastern Mountain Sports®, to a local speed shop or junkyard or other store that is an information center for his particular hobby. He may join a national organization (interest groups ordinarily have one) and get magazines. He finds one or more buddies. They talk shop, stimulate each other.

Depending of the size and resources of the town he lives in, and the nature of his hobby, the youth will go through a period of exploration and discovery that is largely social. He will gradually become aware of the hobby's local support system. To take the example of radio-electronics, in the city of Boston, the support system is roughly this:

High school science teachers probably get the boys started. Encouragement and example may come from grown-up hobbyists, ham radio operators, and so on. Expertise and advice comes from a large community of technical experts, the main center being at MIT. There are schools and training programs: electronics engineering (as at MIT); electronic technician courses (Wentworth Institute, RETS Electronics, ITT, others). In addition there are science fairs for high school students, stores (Radio Shack, with its twenty-seven branches, offers a line of kits for learning), and magazines *(Elementary Electronics, Popular Electronics)*. Boys can join ham radio and citizens band broadcasting clubs.

Overlapping with the hobby's support system are interpersonal networks: people, groups, clubs, stores, offices, adademic departments, school groups, who are aware of each other and who share mutual friends, some of whom are ham operators (or whatever the interest is). If the youth lives in an isolated small town, then there will be no support system, no interpersonal network. He may never find a single colleague. In complete isolation, it must be difficult to sustain interest, learn and grow in an area of work. Superior people have done it. But most of us need at least one friend to mirror our enthusiasm. Also we need to be "up on things," so that we do not go off on a mistaken and unproductive tack.

In a larger city the networks are there to be discovered. Access — getting in — is an all-or-none affair, I suspect. If you are socially backward or unfortunate, you can live for long periods, completely "out of it." But if you make one friend who is within the network, you have in effect discovered the entire network. Organized clubs, hobby-groups and courses make entrance fairly easy.

Youth and young adulthood must generally be a period of discovery. You meet people, discover interests, find out about things in the world and within yourself. I suspect the meeting of people tends to lead to the other kinds of discovery. Being a hobbyist — if you really have some enthusiasm — provides an impetus to the social discovery. You are motivated to seek out the club, the store, the other people. When you meet fellow hobbyists, you have something to share.

How the social discovery develops depends on what the community's resources are; on how socially venturesome the person is; and on what kinds of friendship and intimacy he is capable of. For young unmarrieds, the possibilities must be much greater than for Mom and Dad.

A hypothesis: The mechanical-based hobbies offer a rich and superior exploration period. The youth will be meeting work-oriented teenagers and adults. The tendency is to expand: new people, new things to learn. Also, since the hobby career can spin itself out indefinitely, some vestige of the youthful discovery phase may continue into later life.

————

There are also nonmechanical hobbies and interests such as skiing, surfing, amateur theatricals, gymnastics, horseback, hiking and mountain climbing, being a collector, golf, music, dance, and so on. They do not involve working on projects. The work involved is practicing a technique to get better. Pursued casually, they are fun and recreation. A certain number of teenagers get drawn into serious careers in these.

Performing careers occur in sports, music, theater and dance. The young athlete or musician is fairly dedicated, practices, works hard, develops discipline. It is usually time consuming and absorbs a large portion of his interest and energy.

This huge effort is often motivated (I suspect) by a megalomanic fantasy, by dreams of glory. Some coach or teacher has told him, *"You have talent; you can be a star."* This may be reinforced by some early successes: victories, starring roles, the crowd's applause. I think these careers usually end in tragedy, or at least trail off in disappointment, because of impossibly lofty goals: to be an Olympic swimmer, a football hero, a concert pianist. Professional-level standards of performance which are often learned (I think) in this kind of training also assure fairly chronic disappointment. For example, to play a round of golf or a Debussy prelude merely well enough, acceptably all right, may be nearly impossible because of the young musician's or golfer's too-high standards. Also, the nature of competition in these fields is such that at the end of nearly every campaign, every career, is a climactic defeat.

These careers do have similarities to other serious hobby careers. They are working interests; the youth strives to get better; he is ambitious and he has goals. He goes through an apprentice period; he often must emulate one or more teachers, coaches, older persons. He is part of a local network. These people are an in-group, a brotherhood (despite all the competition and rivalry), by virtue of the common initiation they have gone through: the specialized training, practice and discipline. Also they can appreciate one another's talents. So there is normally group support for his hard work and interest, and a group-based rationale and value system that justifies it. It tends to be very absorbing. A young musician's practicing, plus his musician friends, can be "his life." A serious devotion to surfing and skiing (in season), the team sports, and the other performing careers can be similarly absorbing, and supported by in-group membership. If the career is successful for awhile, the rewards can be enormous.

When Debbie was eight years old, her father enrolled her in the Boston Children's Theatre. She showed promise and was given serious training. By eleven she was playing roles in Children's Theatre productions. By fifteen she had played twenty-one major roles in plays — leads, props director, lighting, and so on. Her large scrapbook shows pictures of a queenly Debbie *(The Fairy Queen)*, an animated Debbie *(Hello Dolly!)*, a mature Debbie *(Mother Goose)*. Now at sixteen she has played summer stock and is becoming known in Greater Boston theater circles. She cannot take high school very seriously. She finds her school mates immature. After her first week with a summer theatrical group she said, "Gee it's good to be with theater people again."

Here is one more example of a serious hobby career that is not performing nor particularly competitive.

Karen went to riding stables for several years and took lessons. She became really serious, was influenced by an admired teacher, and persuaded her parents to lease a fine horse for her. Now she goes to the horse barn after school every day. She cares for her horse, rides, and socializes with the other horse people. On Saturdays she works all day at the barn to pay part of the expenses. She shovels manure and does other horse-related work.

Her parents remark on the dramatic change in her. Formerly a lazy, mocking, dissatisfied teenager, she runs an obstacle course to get fit since she is working to become a good rider. She does her chores and her homework with no prompting; this was part of the agreement when they leased the horse. She says she may become a veterinarian; she talks about getting a summer job with a vet, for the experience. She is working, ambitious, focused, "serious," whereas formerly she was floppy and disaffected. Her parents are mightily impressed.

Horseback careers could be divided into two types: (1) the rich-girl hobby — the girl competes with her horse in shows; the horse, riding togs, and room and board in stables add up to a sizeable expense; (2) the working interest — this is more typical of country youths and girls who grow up with animals. As they get older, they find new opportunities to ride horses: perhaps working for a neighbor, "leading trails" at a stables or dude ranch, or spending a summer at a real ranch out West. City girls (and boys) without wealthy parents, who fall in love with horses, may do what they can to work at the stables *and* work on their parents, as Karen has done.

Horseback has its interpersonal network and its support

system: teachers, stables, breeders, ranchers, and professional associations that regulate the shows and publish newsletters. A Colorado dude ranch (which a friend visited) was staffed by young people from various parts of the country. My friend says they represented two hobby groups. There were "horse people" and "folk dance people." The network provides news of summer jobs. For Karen and young people like her, the payoffs from her interest can be varied and unexpected.

There are other kinds of animal hobbies. In my sample are two girls who show dogs. But horseback, which is simultaneously the love and care of horses, learning to ride, and competition in shows, which offers regular opportunities to socialize with other horse people (in-groups at stables and at shows), seems to have more potential for hobby careers.

HOBBY CAREERS' BENEFITS

One benefit from all serious hobbies might be summed up in the term *focus*. It is illustrated by Karen's dramatic change for the better. Energy is harnessed. Active, turned-on work habits are learned (as opposed to passive, compliant, bored habits often learned in school). I assume that teenagers hunger for grown-up competence. If the youth makes any progress in his (or her) field of interest, he builds competence and feeds his self-esteem. Something must happen, identity-wise. The youth must have an image of realizeable self — pianist, hot rodder, master carpenter like his grandfather, or whatever. Motivation must also come from daily and weekly rewards of the hobby — whether it is the triumphs of the competitive performing careers (as in the case of Debbie), or the satisfactions of projects.

This kind of focus must be an antidote to certain problems of adolescence, as with Karen's improved behavior.[2] This is an empirical question, of course, and might possibly be studied,

---

[2]See for example Erikson's writings on identity strivings and identity diffusion:

Erik H. Erikson, "Growth and Crisis in a Healthy Personality," in C. Kluckhohn, H. Murray, and D. Schneider, eds., *Personality in Nature, Culture and Society* (New York, Alfred A. Knopf, 1955).

Erik H. Erikson, *Identity, Youth and Crisis* (New York, W. W. Norton & Co., 1968).

although it seems to be researchable only to a very limited degree.

Many of the interest groups are adult oriented. The teenager may apprentice to an adult or fraternize with adult hobbyists, or the models he emulates may be adults. (A few interest groups are still very much part of the teen scene; for example, the surfers and the motorbikers.) If the hobby group is not in itself deviant or criminal, then it is probably a "good influence" (from the parents' point of view). This is not always the case. One boy's most admired and accomplished bike-mechanic friend was also a bicycle thief. Depending on the era, some few hobby careers may introduce the boy into a deviant subculture. In my youth this happened to boys who became jazz musicians. But these must be in the minority, and they must be fairly easy to spot.

A serious interest may "keep him out of trouble" because (1) work on the hobby, and social imvolvement with the hobby group, leaves little time or interest for other, more dangerous activities or associations; and (2) the hobby orientation conflicts with deviant orientations.

> "My parents really liked it that I was going to be on the college swim team. They figured I'd have to stay in training. I'd be working out with the other swimmers, swimming laps every day. I couldn't be smoking dope, I couldn't drink or run around nights. They didn't know that that's what the guys did."

It is a research question just how much a sports career (or other kinds of hobby careers) "keeps them off the streets" or "keeps them out of trouble." Perhaps there is research evidence on the effects of sports, but I have been unable to find it.

Another benefit of serious hobby careers is that they can start favorable lines of development. They may lead a teenager out of a bad period, as with the case of Karen. They can "open doors" — either to adult occupations or to opportunities of other kinds. Karen's horse people, Debbie's theater people, wilderness groups, youth hostelers, and so on must act powerfully to encourage kids into new ventures — traveling, taking jobs, trying new things — by providing the example of friends who did it and who tell about it. Similarly, mechanical and scientific groups like the electronics network must draw boys into more advanced work and into new interests. This is really another way of stating the hypothesis about the youthful exploration and discovery period — that it is improved by a serious hobby.

After awhile, some hobby careers come to a dead end. I am thinking particularly of music and competitive sports.

In my case files, the most impressive young people who seem to have the greatest resources, the most useful skills, the widest scope, and the happiest prospects are nearly all serious hobbyists. Most are serious *mechanical* hobbyists. In their lines of development — how they got that way — working on hobbies seems to have played a prominent part. One can ask: which came first? They must be unusual to begin with, in that they did not merely dabble in hobbies, but got deeply involved and made something out of them. What determines whether a teenager will be a dabbler or a serious worker on photography, or ceramics, or cabinet making? I have hypothesized that mechanical aptitude, maybe previous mechanical experience, is a determinant of serious involvement in the hobbies where mechanical work comes into play. (This includes almost everything outside sports and the performing arts.) But there must be other determinants too. Superior personal qualities, already-learned work habits, discipline, motivational sets — these may also be involved. So perhaps an early-childhood development along a good track laid the foundation for these persons' serious hobby careers. However it comes about, the hobbies then act back on the unfolding of the young lives.

Harry's parents work on projects around the home; this is the household style. He must have begun by watching and helping out in small ways. At an early age he was assigned chores. His father is a fixer, worked with his tools around the home, and provided a model. Harry "showed good mechanical sense, a feel for machines," learned to operate power tools, and has now done a great deal of mechanical work. He has also cut off the tip of a finger on the lathe in the basement. He now does a variety of household repairs, yard work, work in the kitchen and various chores. He produces beautiful wooden bowls, lamps, and shelves in the basement woodworking shop.

Harry has had a rich hobby career. It verges on the "boy inventor" pattern which will be described in the *Enterprise*, chapter. With a friend he built gasoline-powered planes and boats; they tried to build an underwater bubble in a nearby lake.

His father says he is a good cooperative work-mate. He is good at "pitching in and helping out." His mother says that Harry has two different styles of working: one for assigned work and chores, and another style for his own projects. He is very disciplined about doing his school work. His approach for homework and chores is to hit the work hard, right now, and get it out of the way. For projects — things that he is working on in the basement — his tendency is to start a lot of them and then nibble at them, so there are many partly finished projects lying around at any one time.

At age ten, Harry decided he wanted to study whales. That has given some career focus to his school work. He aspired to an oceanography program, had to make good grades, learned scuba diving, read oceanography magazines. He went on a school tour to a Newfoundland whaling station.

Harry's two summer jobs have been yard and woods work. He ingratiated a difficult boss; he saved his money. He is big and strong, a high school wrestler. His father says he has shown signs of leadership qualities, but Harry spends little time on social life. He usually has something else to do.

His formidable resources include: the style of working at school and pattern of school success; the rich hobbies and interests and the planning-building style that has grown out of them; and the self-maintenance skills he has learned; not to mention being big and strong, saving his money, the pattern of family helping (a precious gift to his future wife and children); and the opportunities which open up by virtue of his school career and his hobby career.

HOBBIES PREPARE FOR OCCUPATIONS

I believe serious teenage hobbyists are usually working toward an adult career goal. They want to stay with their interest and somehow make a living at it; or (as with Harry) there are multiple interests and an associated career goal. It seldom must work out the way the youths plan it at age ten or twelve or fourteen. But the hobby does sometimes track the youth into an adult occupation, perhaps by a series of steps and shifts. These young people are not the ones who go through a long period of drift and indecision after they leave school. The dithering, false starts, and apparent reluctance to enter the work world which I see in students and exstudents is not a problem for the serious hobbyists. (This of course is an empirical question; in modified form it could be tested.)

The really impressive youth like Harry seem to have so many resources, so much going for them, that their choice of career may be not all that important. They could succeed (so it seems) in many lines of work; they could optimize all manner of life situations. Nowadays job markets are shrinking in many fields. Professional schools are hard to get into. The rewards of professional training are less certain. It is good for a young person to have a range of skills, or a variety of possible things he might do. Preparing to be opportunistic about jobs and careers, not resting all one's hopes on a single plan and program of training, having the wherewithal to do something else if one's life plan falls through — this looks like the best strategy. The young people like Harry, and the "enterprisers" and "managers" I will soon be discussing, seem best prepared for this situation. And this seems partly due to their hobby backgrounds.

THE MANY ADVANTAGES OF MECHANICAL KNOWLEDGE

I would like to sum up the advantages (as I see them) of mechanical ability. Whereas sports are much in the limelight, and music, theater, and dance tend to have high prestige, the reputation of the mechanical arts is unjustifiably low I think. This must have to do with the fact that mechanical occupations are blue collar, lower class. This appears in a number of the case studies. A mechanical son of a mechanic father is loath to follow in his father's footsteps, sometimes the parents discourage him too, for what seem to be status reasons.

Mechanical skills are of course useful skills. If you think of all the things children and teenagers spend their time on, all the years of learning to do things, working, playing and practicing — how much of that investment can actually be cashed in later? When I entered the army I was put to work as a typist. That was my one skill which the army could use. Subsequently, I based an academic career on two core skills learned (partly) in school: reading and writing. All the thousands of hours spent practicing football (in order to become a football hero), shooting baskets, chasing fly balls, working on my golf game, not to mention the time spent at pure recreation, and perhaps ninty percent of the time spent in school: I have realized nothing from this investment. Similarly for much of the work that modern-day children do: the Hebrew classes, the clarinet lessons, the band practice, gym class, civics, hockey practice at 7 AM, and so on.

To return to my own case: My wife would like to live in a charming old Nova Scotia home. We never will, because I am not a fixer. We both would like to have a country place. This is impracticable too; I do not have the self-maintenance skills. During my lifetime, many times I have been confronted by a machine that would not work — a car that wouldn't start, or whatever — and forced to try to cope with it. Mechanical coping is unavoidable, especially when you go to the country or to backward areas. My anthropological fieldwork in the Caribbean and in Spain taught me the importance of mechanical skills in backward countries. Nearly all the underdeveloped parts of the world now have the machines; but they do not have good support and maintenance for them. So the machines break down, and parts and repairmen are often hard to find. Being able to fix the generator, start the outboard motor, get the toilet to flushing again are highly prized skills. Some mechanical ability is the best resource I can think of for around-the-world traveling and adventuring. Jobs should be easy to find along the way.

Similarly for anyone who wishes to retreat to nature, to the country, back to the farm, to homesteading or whatever, there are all sorts of options like this, which are open to mechanical people. Paradoxically, one's dealings with the machines become more intimate with any attempt to escape to more primitive, "natural" living.

If one has no mechanical background and feels that he can learn, one may of course take the leap. It would be interesting to study the success record of modern homesteaders: those that were successful, and those that soon quit, and relate this to previous mechanical knowhow. Having talked with a few homesteaders, I am aware of the lengthy inventory of tools, skills, and knowledge needed to do for yourself on a country place.

So being mechanical means having alternatives, being able to do and have a great many things which otherwise probably would not be feasible.

Finally, to restate two previous points:

• A "mechanical" father, with his wife, can create a working-on-projects life-style in his home. He stands an infinitely greater chance of drawing his son into family helping. He has something to base a work-apprenticeship on. Daughters may also be greatly affected. (This is a testable hypothesis.)

• Finally the *involvement* hypothesis: Nonmechanical people are apt to be discouraged by mechanical problems that most hobbies raise; so they soon quit the hobby, they do not develop it very far. Mechanical people are more apt to persevere and have serious hobby careers.

It is too bad that we do not know more about getting children off to a good start (and preventing a bad start) in the mechanical area. As learning to read and write (from age six) is a core skill for school success and all the careers that flow from that, the mechanical is another core skill. Many good lines of development and opportunities that I have been reviewing seem (to a large extent) to depend on getting off to a good start — or at least avoiding a bad start — in mechanical work.

FACILITATING MECHANICAL WORK AND HOBBIES

All but about five of my mechanical people started their

careers in childhood. They learned in their homes and neighborhoods, from their fathers and other persons who were doing
this work. They took advantage of manual training courses in
school, and later they got into interest groups and organized
hobbies.

What can be done for children who do not start out in
naturally-occurring mechanical milieux?

• Certain placements might be arranged (as suggested in
Chap. 7). An old man who is a putterer might be happy to have
a child follow him around, "help" him, and receive instruction. Or the child might visit a home where mechanical work is
being done. This placement could be casual dropping-in, in
the neighborhood, or it might be with a relative. This is suggested as a way of compensating for no mechanical background
in the home. I know of no mechanical people who got their
start this way. However, several did begin — not in their own
homes — but by observing and learning in the neighborhood,
or in the village, or from a friend. Certain boys seem to find
their way into mechanical careers all by themselves. They get
interested in something — maybe they have a friend who is
doing it — and they find a way to learn and get started. Then
they are on their way.

• The value of manual training classes depends on the
school the child attends. The classes can start in the fourth,
seventh, or tenth grades, and have high- or low-quality
training. How worthwhile are manual training courses all by
themselves, if the child has not done other mechanical work at
home or with friends? Perhaps they are mainly valuable as a
supplement to the home training, a second step in the boy's
education.

• As far as hobby groups are concerned: some of these can,
all by themselves, introduce an older child into a hobby, socialize him and teach him. Electronics is organized in this
fashion, with the Radio Shacks and other stores, ham radio
clubs, and so on. In the junior high school years, a child might
be recruited into electronics via this route. Other branches of
mechanical work are not organized in this way. Work on auto-
mobiles is an example. For this, you really need the home
training. If you do not get it, and cannot arrange to learn from

someone informally, then you have to wait for high school. Some high schools, I understand, offer worthwhile training in automotive mechanics.

How important is it, that a child receives mechanical training? I don't know, of course. Several men in the sample did not start until they were adults, and then they learned fast. I have the impression that this is unusual, but I have no good statistical evidence to check this against.

If mechanical work starts in childhood, then it gives an early jumping-off point for interests and hobbies (as just described). And the possible gains from these are — again — focus; maybe apprenticing to and modeling after a working adult; joining a work-oriented interest group; perhaps a lower likelihood of certain teenage problems and "trouble"; maybe tracking into an occupation; and a period of youthful discovery which is enriched.

Chapter 12

MANAGING AFFAIRS

ONE aspect of growing up is acquiring experience by doing thing for ourselves, going out into the world on our own.

We start out as children, and at home and at school most of the arrangements are made for us. Kindergartners are even lined up and sent to the bathroom en masse. "Gaining some experience" means learning to make some of our own arrangements, and not simply following the procedures that parents and teachers have worked out for us. I can remember some of my first ventures: paying the barber for my haircut (forgetting to pay him and being called back), trying to find my way around the school building (bewildered and lost in the crowded hallways, and noticing that other children found their way around with ease). I was rather backward, having been sheltered and protected. Other children were more precocious.

As children grow into adolescents, they learn to find their way, go into the city by themselves, take the bus, make transactions in stores. They learn to keep appointments, meet deadlines, and remember what they have to do.

My university students still forget, even though they have had years of experience in school, meeting deadlines and following instructions. There really is a great deal to learn before one is performing at the responsible-adult level. In their late teens, some people are still losing their mittens and coming a day late for their appointments.

Along with learning to be a reliably scheduled person, one learns the ins and outs of informal agreements. "Meet me at the corner at five o'clock." "Take my paper route for the week of July 23." "Let us go partners in this."

Mark's paper route was his first work experience, and he did remarkably well. But he made one disastrous mistake. When he went away on vacation the little boy he chose as his substitute did not deliver the paper every day. Either there had been a mix-up in the arrangements (that is, the agree-

156

ment had not been made clear to both Mark and the substitute), or he had chosen an irresponsible boy.

Mark showed bad judgment. Perhaps if he goes through more learning trials like this he will profit by experience, get feedback from such mistakes, and acquire more seasoned judgment.

As we grow up our affairs become more complex and the demands get heavier: punctuality, running by the clock, depending on others ("You do this and I'll do that" arrangements between people); keeping records, a bankbook, an appointment calendar, reminder lists; meeting deadlines. We have obligations to school (show up on time; get in the assignments); to job (show up on time; do, reliably, whatever you are expected to do; coordinate with others workers); to home ("Pick me up at five o'clock"). We thread the maze of traffic, do the shopping, plan ahead — the next week, the school term. Bureaucracies must be dealt with: forms filled out at registration and income tax time, regulations complied with, red tape coped with in dealings with government offices. If we move into business or into managerial positions, we ourselves become part of the bureaucratic realm. We may have to learn about committees, running a formal meeting, business management and legal niceties. We must (in such a position) try to become procedures-wise.

The demands are heavy for businessmen. They create opportunities for themselves by being willing to take on more complexities of this sort. This is also true for managers and office holders, and for people in the professions. The demands are heavier in big cities. One can scale communities according to how much they require and how forgiving they are toward people of limited competence: small town — Halifax — Boston — New York City. The demands increase with modernization. Underdeveloped countries, cities as well as villages, tend to require little in the way of punctuality, scheduling, and reading and understanding directions (at least this seemed to be true where I have traveled, in Spain and in the Caribbean.)

The more you are willing and able to take on, the greater your scope in modern society. The more things you can do:

fight the city, get things from bureaucracies, run a business or work in politics; have a managerial career; travel; and even job hunt effectively. There are attendant risks, of course. You can be "caught in the rat race," trapped in an impossible managerial position. Businesses (and households) may fail because affairs become so complex and disorderly as to get out of control.

So much for the delineation of the dimension, *managing affairs*.

I will be describing some young people who developed very fast, as a result of holding offices, working, and traveling. The cases raise some issues — relevant to parents — about the value of such experiences.

• What benefit is it, in the long run, to get a fast start in managing your own affairs? Eventually everyone learns to do it anyway. What good is it to be an experienced and seasoned teenager?

I think there are many kinds of fast starts. My case studies say: sometimes at least it turns out very well. Judy and Babette and Irv and company are so experienced, they seem capable of handling many situations. One has the feeling that they would not be misled and would not make mistakes, like less mature teenagers might. (This is an empirical question, of course: whether early experience helps avoid later mistakes and, if so, what kind.) Also, some of the officeholders' teenage activities are leading right into adult professions. Beyond that, if they had not had fast starts, they certainly would have missed out on a lot.

• A second issue is: Just what is the meaning of "experience" to immature children and adolescents? They might very well not "learn lessons" from their "mistakes" in the way we would expect. To return to the example of Mark, who let the wrong boy substitute for him on his paper route: After some experiences like this maybe he will learn how to make arrangements. Perhaps he will develop more seasoned judgment. Then again, maybe he won't. Teenage preoccupations, "mental static," may interfere with the normal perception of events and with learning from them. I think that some youths are distracted by their teenage preoccupations, and others are not. Teenagers who are so afflicted probably go through phases; they are probably capable of learning some lessons and not others.

How can this kind of trouble be minimized? My own guess — which must be predictable by this time — is that the answer is early maturity, as a result of work and responsibility starting in childhood.

Making allowance for a certain amount of mental static and inability to learn, I would propose the following hypothesis. One determinant of a teenager's maturity and sophistication is the number and variety of real-world situations in which he has had to make his own arrangements. If he has had much experience, he has probably been put in situations in which he not only made arrangements, but was also held accountable, had some responsibility. This will tend to make him more reliable, more realistic in his planning, more seasoned in his judgments (as opposed to being "silly," unreliable, feckless).

• A third issue has to do with freedom and autonomy. Children cannot be sheltered and chaperoned forever. They have to learn from experience, "make their own mistakes." But this is risky. The mistakes can have serious consequences: an auto accident, a pregnancy, school dropout, a disastrous marriage, a police record. Or, put in terms of lines of development and teenage careers: It can take good turns or bad.

A youth acquires experience by managing for himself. But he cannot do this without risking serious mistakes.

Give responsibility along with discretionary powers is part of the answer, I think. The precocious teenagers who seem to have turned out so well — Judy and Babette and Irv and the rest — started as family helpers, babysitters, paperboys, volunteer workers. They were put in accountable, adult-like roles. They were not simply given freedom to have fun and adventures with friends (although some of them had quite a lot of this kind of freedom too). If the emphasis is on responsibility rather than peer group fun, then perhaps the odds are improved: that growth in wisdom, "profiting by experience," will keep ahead of the risk of disastrous mistakes.

Another part of the answer may be: start them early. Early competence, early habits of work and accountability, can be the foundation for the sorts of impressive careers we see in the case studies — the officeholders, world travelers, serious hobbyists, enterprisers, and altruistic persons. And perhaps teenagers who are more experienced and seasoned than their peers at any particular age — fourteen or sixteen or eighteen — are less apt to be taken in by harebrained schemes.

Aside from these general issues, parents may also question the benefits of particular kinds of teenage activities. Is hitchhiking really worth the risk? In the long run, is the president of the student council, the organizer of the senior prom, the Hi-Y leader, benefitted by this work? Those who continue on to administrative careers: perhaps they were manager types anyway, and would have done so without this experience in high school.

PREMATURE MATURITY: THROWN OUT INTO THE STREETS AT A TENDER AGE

Between ages five and eight, Judy lived in a Toronto flat with her three brothers. Her father was gone; her mother was working. Part of the time the mother was in the hospital, and the children managed for themselves. They gathered bottles along the highway, shopped for groceries, prepared their meals, agreed on household chores, roamed the city (and occasionally got lost), slept close together when the heat was turned off, lived on mustard sandwiches when money ran out.

By the time their mother took them back to Cape Breton to their grandparents' home, they had had years of experience in caring for themselves in the city. Their grandparents insisted on "proper supervision" for the children. Judy had the novel experience of going back to a more childlike status.

Judy says, "Never before had I seen so many rules and regulations. People saw to it that I had a regular bedtime and bath day — things which I had always taken for granted and did when the mood struck me. They saw that I ate regularly and dressed 'properly,' in fact, they took over my life's organization almost completely. For the first time in four years my care and welfare was taken out of my hands and put into the hands of my grandparents."

Judy, as a result of her early seasoning in Toronto (and the way the children and the mother met the crisis), was extraordinarily precocious in managing her own affairs. It was the foundation for an amazing career, which I will return to again.

Being thrown out into the streets at a tender age can be educational. In Judy's case it was a brilliant success. Several other people in the sample fended for themselves in Toronto and New York, and they also seem to have benefitted by the experience. But they are not such extreme cases. They were older, and they were not left completely on their own.

Mary Engel and her colleagues studied Boston shoeshine boys.[1] The children who survived in this fiercely competitive world were precocious in a somewhat different way: street wise, rather dishonest and predatory. (The Artful Dodger in Dickens' *Oliver Twist* comes to mind.) There are some formidable youths in Mary Engel's sample.

No doubt early street exposures have disastrous effects for some children. But they did not find their way into Engel's sample, or mine.

We are really considering two variables here:

• How early in life do on-your-own experiences start?

• How challenging, dangerous, demanding are they? How much self-reliance and arrangements-making is called for? Are you getting a haircut in Lunenburg or shining shoes in downtown Boston?

Judy, and Engel's boys, represent the extreme on both variables: fairly total self-reliance in a dangerous big city, at a very early age.

A big-city exposure must give a great boost to this kind of learning. It is informative, stimulating. You must look sharp and be alert. However, many city children are chaperoned and protected (because of the dangers) until they are fairly old. Since they do not plunge into city life — like Judy did — they learn less. A woman who grew up in New York says, "I learned to keep my nose in a book. Going places on a

---

[1]Mary Engel, Gerald Marsden, and Sylvia Pollock, "Child Work and Social Class," *Psychiatry, 34*:140-155, 1971.

bus or in the subway, I kept my nose in a book and never looked up."

OFFICE HOLDING

About fifteen people in the sample had managerial careers in their teens, as a result of doing volunteer work.

> Babette grew up in Cape Breton in the Sydney area. She describes herself as "quiet, with few friends," until she became active in Young Christian Students (YCS) at about grade ten. She went to a leadership training camp where, she says, she "learned to speak out in groups." She participated in a series of money-raising drives and other ventures, helped train new workers, and evidently began to develop some managerial skills. She also became part of the youth worker and volunteer establishment in Sydney. First she became friends with the four salaried adults who ran the YCS Federation in Sydney; they introduced her to the rest of the network. At age eighteen, she was put in charge of a shift at Metrocenter Helpline in Sydney. This further widened her contacts. Babette's work history combines volunteer work and paid work on social service projects, all in Cape Breton. She has worked on several surveys, helped set up youth hostels, organized workshops and public relations programs, run a Helpline, been in charge of the Metrocenter building, and been a Headstart worker. Her committee memberships include executive secretary of the Cape Breton Hostel Association, and member of the Cape Breton Advisory Board for Opportunities for Youth. This is really a very truncated work history; many of her activities have been left out.

In managerial careers, as with mechanical careers, one thing leads to another. Once the process is started, it gathers momentum. Once Babette had been identified as a willing and reliable worker, and had received some leadership training in YCS, she was "called on" to do various administrative tasks; evidently it went well enough so that she was called on again. Operating in a small city, she quickly got to know — and became known by — other workers in youth programs, volunteer programs, and social service agencies. This is an explanation (of sorts) of the social aspect of her career, which might be characterized as "Big frog in a small pond." As to her actual performance, the operations she managed, the skills she learned:

> Babette says about herself, "I am an organizer. I enjoy work; especially complicated work projects that I have to do efficiently. I start with loose ends and work toward the middle. I am a 'list' person. No matter what I. do I have at least three or four lists for it; scratching out, adding and then making a new list. For a simple example, I organize the dishes when I wash them. Everything must be cleared off the table and put on the right side of the counter, the table must be washed off and the stove cleared before I even start to wash."

> Babette was the hardworking older sister in a large Cape Breton family which lived (part of the time) in the country with wood stove and garden. This provided the early background to her career. Caring for others and being accountable in the home, handling a work overload by being very organized, altruistic tendencies — then church work, volunteer work, doing her duties well, and taking responsibility — and she was on her way.

This seems like a natural development. And "coping by organizing" — the style of handling a work overload by being superorganized — characterizes a number of women and girls in my sample, each of whom started out in the overworked elder sister role, and then went on to managerial careers. This is a coping style and a line of development which is familiar to me now. However, few teenagers (elder sister or not) do become managers; many females do not respond to the challenge of heavy housework and child care by becoming very organized. Also, as an explanation for Babette's managerial career, this is only a rudimentary beginning, since it does not examine what she actually did on her jobs. Part of the credit evidently goes to Young Christian Students for giving her a start.

I understand that a number of churches have leadership training programs — workshops and training camps for teenagers (and others) who have already become active workers in young people's groups and in other church volunteer programs. They give formal training in leadership skills for young people who are emerging as people who can be leaders, who are willing to work and give their time, who are responsible and motivated. How to lead a discussion, run a meeting, coordinate a project, tell people what to do, and the assurance that comes with practice — these, I assume are the kinds of "leadership skills" that are learned.

Few teenagers step forward to do the church work and other volunteer work. Of those few volunteers, some gravitate to office holding and committee work, and others never get managerial experience. (They are the candy stripers, the Meals on Wheels drivers, the volunteer workers in mental hospitals and nursing homes.) Teenagers who volunteer for work that gives managerial opportunities — if they prove themselves reliable and willing to work — are moved ahead from one job to the next. Like Babette, they are introduced to the local service establishment. This can lead to a self-contained career within a single organization (I know one man who has spent his entire life, from childhood, with the YMCA), or to a ministerial or counseling career, or to more varied managerial experience, which might be used in a number of ways. (In many walks of life it helps to know about committees, know how to run a formal business meeting, how to organize a money-raising drive or a social event.) Perhaps it tends to lead to executive positions in business and government. This might be studied.[2]

[Jean, our next case, worked in Hi-Y.] "I joined it because my friends were getting into it. Hi-Y took in high school students and put them to work raising money for various causes. Our Halifax Hi-Y had about twenty clubs. Each club had about twenty members. I was a rather shy member of a club called 'Vogethia' (Greek word, meaning 'to aid') during my first year. By the middle of that year I had stopped being shy and retiring. I represented my club on the Fellowship Council, which was the 'head' committee for the Hi-Y. I learned about parliamentary procedures, public relations for the money-raising drives, finance, and Hi-Y politics; and I

---

[2]Harold Wilensky gives evidence of a correlation between business leadership and volunteer work (for adults). "Orderly Careers and Social Participation: The Impact of Work History on Social Integration in the Middle Class," *American Sociological Review*, 26:521-539, 1961.

got more confident.

"More and more, I found I was organizing more complex activities. I handled a number of massive clothing drives, to collect clothes for needy people. These drives required a lot of advance planning and 'clearing' with the proper city officials.

"When I reached the eleventh grade, I spent part of each day doing Hi-Y work. By that time I was president of my club; I was vice-president of the Fellowship Council. Also, I served with adult officers on the board of directors of the YMCA. I was going to meetings all the time. Working on the board, I was introduced into the adult managerial world. I learned the language of fiscal years, deficits, expenditures, budgeting, and architectural plans."

When I pressed Jean to try to explain just why she had been drawn into the work (since Hi-Y also had its social aspect, and other teenagers joined for the dances and the get-togethers), she said that originally she had joined merely because her friends were doing it. Then she got singled out as a worker. (Many of the kids evidently were not workers, or proved themselves unreliable, or did not take an active part in the meetings.) Why was she "a worker?" She said that was the way she was trained at home, to be very conscientious. And she was "idealistic" — she believed in the moneyraising drives. As far as speaking up in the meetings was concerned, if you did not get involved and do some of the talking yourself, the meetings were terribly boring. (This must be a principle that applies to all meetings, in university, government, or clubs.)

During the period in which Jean was learning and gaining new responsibilities and becoming an important officeholder it was rather exciting. But the main reason she was drawn in was: she was called on to do a few things, and she did them; as a result, she was called on more. "Once started, it never stopped." (Once you prove you will do the job satisfactorily, you are called on again and again, until you refuse, demure, or prove yourself unreliable. This must be another general rule for volunteering and committee assignments.)

When she left high school, Jean cut off her involvement with Hi-Y. This ended her managerial career (up to now, at age twenty). Her subsequent volunteer work, with the Nova Scotia

Museum, has been of the non-office-holding variety.

What did the Hi-Y experience add up to? From being shy and retiring, Jean learned to speak up at meetings, even to take charge. She traveled to conferences and had experience talking business to adults. She learned something of the various aspects of administrative work. She knows she can do it (and I suspect she will be called on to do it again). She must have grown in self-confidence and in sense of mastery in many areas.

In the next case, volunteer work with several youth agencies and Jewish organizations has been woven into a whirlwind schedule: school, jobs, a heavy load of family helping, and volunteer work all done simultaneously. Irv's managerial career includes:

- Youth leadership training at a Jewish summer camp;
- A year at the Institute for Youth Leaders from Abroad in Jerusalem;
- Administrative work within Young Judea;
- Committee membership on several other Jewish organizations, and on the Halifax Child and Youth Action Council.

Whereas Babette's small network in which she became established was social service in Sydney, Irv's has been Jewish organizations. They gave him quick access to managerial jobs, training, contacts, a springboard for his career.

Irv is a high-energy person, an enterpriser. This must be one reason why he can give his time as a volunteer. Like other enterprisers, he has a surplus of energy. On the other hand, experience at running things — in a volunteer capacity — has given more scope to his enterprise career.

Will Irv go on to some high-level executive position, or to a complicated life in which he sits on various committees and boards of directors? Irv would say no. He has renounced his ambition to be a social worker; now he wants to be a primal psychotherapist. I hope to check back with him several years from now.

The final case is David — a fat boy who was not good in athletics, who craved recognition, and finally got some as an athletic manager in a canoe club.

"I realized I would not go far as a paddler, so I looked

around for other things to do. When I was sixteen, I got my first chance. The head coach of the club noticed me hanging around waiting for my friends to finish their practice. He asked me if I would like to help him by timing some of the crews and helping out during regattas. Soon I found that I was completely accepted by everyone. . . . The next summer I was asked to serve on the service committee, which was responsible for running the weekly teenage dances. During the same summer I was asked by the paddling chairman to serve on his committee. For one reason or another I ended up in charge of the social committee when I was eighteen — a position I held for the next four years. During that time we raised some five thousand dollars for the club, and I had a direct say in how the money was spent. My work on the paddling committee consisted mainly of being club whipper-in, which meant that I was responsible for getting the crews to the line on time with their proper lane numbers . . . and being club representative on the Maritime Division, which is the local governing body of the sport of paddling."

In the following years, David held a series of offices: youngest member of the club's executive committee, team manager at the Canadian championships, referee at regattas, judge at regattas, member of the club's social and membership committees, and Atlantic Division registrar and statistician. He has traveled to nine Canadian championships and has, needless to say, made many contacts in canoe circles. He hopes to make his career in sports administration.

As in the cases of Babette, Jean and Irv, David answered a call for willing workers, proved himself reliable, and grew in importance. Like Irv and Babette, family helping is prominent in his background, both farm work and child care. He had the need for recognition and the necessary personal qualities; the canoe club offered a managerial career to him.

To return to the question, was the administrative involvement worthwhile? Was it worth it? The answer certainly seems to be yes in the case of Dave. He must have been sorely in need of some prop to his self esteem; he seems to have gotten enormous gratification from his work. For Babette, Jean, and Irv, the answer depends partly on what they eventually do in life;

on just what, precisely, their office-holding experiences have prepared them *for.* We do not know if they will go on to do more administrative work (although I think it is fairly safe to assume that they will, at some point in their lives), nor do we know how much help their teenage experiences will prove to be. (Perhaps they are all managerial types who were destined for office holding, sooner or later, in any case.) All we know is that they had meteoric careers in their teens, as a result of this work; they appear to be developing beautifully.

Probably, if we only knew, some office holding — for some teenagers — turns out to be trivial as experience. An example from my own case is president of the student council in high school. Other such experiences — for some teenagers — turn out to be strategic. They lead to a favorable line of development (as in the way David got started, timing the canoes; or Babette, working with YCS); or they can be "cashed in" in later life.

Does office holding in the teens prepare for later administrative careers? It certainly is not necessary. Some successful administrators never do this sort of work until they are adults. But it must be helpful; not only for future office-holding, but also for managing one's own affairs.

David, Irv, Babette, Jean, and my other teenage managers got different kinds of administrative experience. David's was business-manager work: selling the tickets, making arrangements for meets with other officials, keeping records and files, handling a budget. The other three supervised and coordinated people on various drives and projects: told people where to meet, what to do, and where to go. All four learned something about formal meetings that run by procedural rules. They also worked in smaller, informal committees. They helped decide on points of policy. To some extent, they were in on the running of organizations.

The application of this kind of experience to later life is fairly obvious, I think. As a professor in a university, I know how important committee work and formal meetings are. How esteemed you are, by your colleagues, is influenced by your performance in committees and meetings, because this is where they see you in action. Businessmen, community workers, and probably most professional people likewise display themselves to their peers in these settings. And of course administrative effectiveness depends (partly) on being skilled in committees and meetings.

Business management, the sort of training David received, would be useful for almost everybody. Competence in this realm is important for running a household and managing any sort of office.

Supervising a staff, managing a drive or campaign, making arrangements for a function, and telling people what to do: a number of benefits should come from this. Aside from the ego-gratification to a teenager who is hungering for grown-up status, there are lessons in interpersonal relations and in making arrangements. These arrangements are more complex than the "Meet me at the corner at five o'clock" agreements between two friends. They should mark a step up in sophistication.

Bureaucratic procedures are probably the most difficult, unpleasant, intimidating, and important kind of administrative work: filling out forms, reading instructions, doing what you have to do to get satisfaction from the registrar's office, or the tax office, or from an insurance company, or a large hospital, or from various government departments. I think the teenage offices are weakest in this kind of training; but they offer some exposure to it.

Experience like this can be a springboard to enterprising careers. I would guess that the steps in the process go something like this:

Successful exposures to this kind of work give you confidence, as well as teaching you how to do things.

Being more confident, you are more apt to get into new ventures and take on new offices. (After all, you have done similar things before.)

This combination — willingness to tackle new projects and lessons learned and contacts made — opens doors. The more you are willing and able to take on, in the way of complex arrangements, record keeping and fiscal management, a crowded appointments calendar, reading forms and instructions and learning bureaucratic procedures in order to get things done — then the more things are possible for you. You can become involved in politics, or business, or the more demanding administrative jobs. You are better able to travel, seize various opportunities, "get into things," have new experiences.

Some of the enterprising careers (in the next chapter) were helped along by teenage office holding. But other enterprisers never did this. Their own individual projects, business ventures, and hobbies and travels took its place. Office holding looks like one of several springboards to an enterprise career.

Another career type that emerges from the officeholders' case studies is *coping-by-organizing*. Babette, and a few other girls, start out by carrying a heavy workload in the home. In high school, they get into organizations, plays, and all kinds of activities. Then they go into jobs and volunteer work. They learn to handle their chronic overload by being very scheduled, keeping notes and lists, and becoming hyperefficient; and this pattern continues into adulthood.

FAMILY HELPING AND MANAGERIAL EXPERIENCE

Most of the managers began as children, helping out in the home. The unusual personal qualities — that made them take up volunteer work and do it well — very likely were fostered by this early work training. David cared for younger siblings and did farm work. Irv became the man of the house at the age of twelve, and he cared for an aged grandmother for several years. Judy was a latchkey child at ages five to eight, and she did heavy, wood stove housework afterward. Babette helped care for a large family. Only Jean got her conscientious habits in some other way. Similarly for the other managers whom I have not mentioned: most of them did much work in the home.

Returning to how we learn to manage our own affairs — how we begin, as children, with the arrangements made for us, and then we gradually learn to do for ourselves — the elder sisters, farm children, and other working children begin the transition earlier. They shift over to join the team of adults that is doing the work, running the home, and making decisions. Farm children hear the family business discussed at the dinner table. Elder sisters are put in the position of making parental decisions. Children who shift over to the team of responsible adults are sent on errands, they go to the store, pay the deliveryman, watch over the younger children in public places, and are in on consultations over household projects and repairs. So in any review of how we learn to manage our own affairs, family helping should not be ignored.

I would like to cite one more case, the touching story of Averill, who came to manage the family business.

She grew up in a small Cape Breton town, the spoiled baby sister in a family of nine children. (She had one younger brother.) Her parents ran a small store and a trailer court. When she was twelve years old, her remaining older sister left home, and Averill's age of responsibility began. She did some housework and baby-sitting. She began to help in the store. Evidently both her parents were having long periods of illness, and more and more of the work was shifted over to her. By age thirteen, she was doing all the housework and minding the store on weekends. At fourteen she also sold greeting cards. When she was fifteen her father died. She was beginning to learn the trailer court business too. When she was seventeen her mother died. Averill was alone and completely in charge — of the store, the trailer court, the house, and her little brother.

"My major work would be running our store. I ran the business with no boss and had to do everything myself. Gradually I learned to do the books and make out orders." [I remarked that she did a lot.] "Not really. You get used to it and learn it gradually. My mum had been sick before and we had to pitch in.

"Running a store makes you realize the value of money and how to spend it wisely. . . . The responsibility of the business was on my shoulders, and if I made a mistake I had to be able to account for it.

"Working in a store was interesting because you meet people of all descriptions and you learn how to handle them when there are problems. . . . I became used to talking to people of all ages and I found the older people interesting, which I believe is unusual for a teenager."

[I probe for how she learned to be a responsibility-taker in the first place. She replies, in effect, that her parents were good teachers.] "I was taught to feel good when I had accomplished something during the day. My parents always made a point of appreciating us for the work we did."

Averill did not manage the store for very long. She and an older brother, who was a nonworking partner, could not agree. The business was sold and she went off to university.

PAID JOBS

Reading over the fifty-odd case studies that mention teenage jobs (not counting baby-sitting), I am struck by the menial, limited nature of the work. Teenagers, when they are able to find employment at all, get the dregs of the job market. Paperboy, yard work, car washing, harvest hand, dishwasher, chambermaid, casual day laborer, routinized production line work: low-paid, low-skill, monotonous jobs which go begging after the adult labor force has had its pick. Most of the work is short-duration summer jobs. University students get the best of it. High school students get what is left. Under sixteen youth may baby-sit, deliver newspapers, caddy, or search for other menial jobs that escape the minimum-age laws.

The educational value of these jobs appears to be rather limited. Any one of them must present a few new "lessons" to be learned, some "hard knocks" perhaps, a little "seasoning" and "experience." But I think they offer less than does child care, or farm work, or serious hobbies, or office holding. There are a few exceptional jobs that seem to offer a lot. But these tend to involve hobbies (as with teenage musicians' careers) or develop out of family helping (as with teenagers who assume responsibility in a family business), or be the reward for volunteer work (as with the managers' careers).

Most jobs are routinized — a stereotyped work situation, a few work operations performed over and over, as with work on a factory assembly line. Informants describe the initial challenge of a new job, followed by boredom once the job has been learned. The jobs with more diversity and responsibility, with more "in" them to be learned, are of course reserved for adults (and usually the better-educated adults at that). Adult workers make this same complaint — that their jobs soon exhaust their challenge and become routine.[3] However this must be even more true for teenagers' jobs.

Nevertheless, the summer jobs and part-time jobs must play their part in teenagers' education. Although most individual jobs seem to offer little, it is, of course, impossible to know for sure; and a youth's overall work history must add up to something.

It is my guess that part-time jobs are most educational if the youth changes jobs frequently. I say this, assuming that what there is "in" a new job, in the way of lessons to be learned, will be quickly used up.[4] This would be especially true for routinized jobs. The learning curve might look something like this:

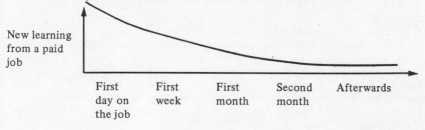

Figure 2.

The most impressive, active youths in my sample tended to have many jobs, and they combined them with hobbies, volunteer work and travel. Jobs permitted travel; they were an occasion for a youth to strike out on his own. There was a reciprocal relationship between jobs and other activities: one thing leading to another. Contacts made in volunteer work led

[3]Studs Terkel, *Working* (New York, Avon Books, 1975).
[4]Psychological studies show that personality change is most pronounced just after people enter a new situation. Similarly for studies of attitude change among college students: Most of the change occurs in the first several months of the freshman year. Glen H. Elder, *Adolescent Socialization and Personality Development* (New York, Rand McNally & Co., 1968), p. 10.

to jobs (as with the case of Babette). The same was true for some of the hobbies (as with horseback and music and mechanical work).

In other words, paid jobs add scope and opportunity, for a youth to develop in a responsible-autonomous-enterprising direction. The recent trend to raise the legal working age and remove teenagers from paid jobs cuts down the opportunity.* It goes along with the dwindling of farm work and work within the home. It must contribute to delayed maturity.

These seem to be the main types of lessons that can be learned in paid jobs:

1. Many of the jobs are extremely arduous. They are a test of a boy's endurance. If he sticks with the job he learns he can do something which many other people probably could not endure. For example, a morning paperboy who rises regularly at 5 AM knows that many of his friends could not keep to this schedule; nor, probably, could his own mother. Similarly

---

*I know something about the laws that keep teenagers from working in Canada and in the United States. The situation is much worse in the United States. In the United States, teenagers can do less. They have to wait until an older age to do it; and the legal liability for people who employ them is complex and vaguely menacing. The specific laws *against* hiring a youth for a particular job until he reaches a certain age are just part of the problem. The ramified consequences of hiring teenagers legally — the government regulations to be complied with (such as those of OSHA, the Occupational Health and Safety Administration), forms to be filled out, and complications to the employer's insurance coverage — must often make it too risky and too much trouble to employ teenagers. According to an Indiana accountant, "If farmers knew all the ways they become liable when they hire kids, they would never do it. The only reason that some of them still do hire kids is that they don't know all the laws."

Laws and regulations have accumulated, many of them in the interests of workers' own health and safety, until teenagers can do less and less. The laws strangle opportunity.

Most employers would rather not risk hiring teenagers. Even in some situations where there is no law against it, it is safer not to take the chance. There may be a law they do not know about, or they might find complications with their insurance, or it is too much trouble to find out.

If anything is to be done about this, a good place to start might be a legal study to discover just what this legal tangle consists of. The study might address itself to questions such as these: (1) What, exactly are the laws, regulations, insurance liability, and red tape that prevent employers from hiring teenagers? (2) As a guideline to employers (and government programs) that want to try to employ teenagers anyway, how do you go about this? (3) What might be done to increase job opportunities, by eliminating some of these restrictive laws and regulations? What changes might be easiest to make, which would make the most difference in freeing up jobs?

for harvest hands, tobacco pickers, corn detasselers, workers in packing houses and warehouses and laundries and kitchens, and on assembly lines, where the eight hours seem like an eternity. The lesson here must be in the nature of a boost to self-esteem, an upgrading of the self-image, reassurance that one is no longer a child. Passing such a test of manliness may be very important to some youths.[5] Primitive societies used to arrange such tests for their adolescents.[6] Some teenage jobs, along with army basic training, may offer a partial substitute for the trials and ordeals of the tribal initiation ceremonies.

Not all jobs are arduous, of course. There are also "fun jobs," and "nothing jobs" that make no real demands on the youth.

2. Jobs can be scaled according to how demanding they are of reliability, dependability, remembering to do this-and-that with such regularity that your boss can count on you. Some jobs' requirements are fairly simple. You need merely show up on time, and follow a simple routine which is easily learned. The work gang, production line jobs tend to be of this sort, I think. The youth works along with a group, and the reliability demands are no greater than what he has already learned in school. On-your-own jobs tend to be more demanding, I think. The youth may have to make novel and complex arrangements, to keep an appointment calendar and reminder lists, and to perform at a higher level if he is not to "forget" and fail to perform some of his duties.

In my sample, the jobs of storekeeping and commercial musician seemed to have the most difficult reliability demands. I would also rate the job of morning paperboy as above average. The paperboy's responsibilities are roughly this. He has to

[5]Erik H. Erikson, "Growth and Crisis in a Healthy Personality," in C. Kluckhohn, H. Murray, and D. Schneider, eds., *Personality in Nature, Culture and Society* (New York, Alfred A. Knopf, 1955).

Erik H. Erikson, *Identity, Youth and Crisis* (New York, W. W. Norton & Co., 1968).
[6]John W. M. Whiting, Richard Kluckhohn, and Albert Anthony, "The Function of Male Initiation Ceremonies at Puberty," in E. E. Maccoby, T. M. Newcomb, and E. L. Hartley, eds., *Readings in Social Psychology* (New York, Holt, Rinehart and Winston, 1958).

wake up, every morning, no matter how he feels, how little sleep he has had, or how bad the weather, and go out into the inhospitable predawn. He has to remember his route. To give good service, he must fold the paper and place it well, in the customer's porch or doorway. He collects from customers and keeps his simple financial records. He must also make an occasional business arrangement, of the you-do-this-and-I'll-do-that sort, with a substitute or with his route manager.

Jobs like this are training youths for adult-like responsibility-demands. A successful paperboy is reliable enough to hold many grown-up jobs.

3. A number of people spoke of "learning the value of money" on their jobs. This particular lesson really turns out to be three or four different kinds of lessons.

• For one thing, there is the simple equation: a dollar equals so many minutes of boredom, monotony, privation, and hot-dusty-sweaty-heavy work on the job. This seems to inspire some youths to conserve their money and make their expenditures count for something, but for others it does not have this effect.

• Then there is "learning the value of money" in the sense of belated appreciation for the things that your parents buy for you. A working teenager may begin to recognize that this same equation applies to his father (to some extent), for his clothes, his college education, things he wants such as a car, as well as for regular family expenses.

• Some jobs require that the youth "handle money." The bookkeeping may be rudimentary, as it is for a paperboy, or it may be more advanced, as with the girl who managed her family's store, did the buying, paid deliverymen, kept the cash register, and took inventory.

• Some youths work to help pay for their university educations. This can start a favorable line of development, leading to a businesslike approach to university studies. It seems to have these components:

The youth has a large personal investment in college success and (looking beyond it) a good career start, since he is paying for it with his many hours of hard work at summer jobs. He is less disposed to "fool around;" and he is more inclined to look seriously at the career payoff of any course of study. (These two hypotheses could be tested.)

The menial summer jobs are a yearly reminder: "I don't want to be stuck in a life like this, like these other people I am working with." The jobs are further inspiration to work hard at school. They provide seasoning to tough employment conditions, and they give a benchmark for comparison with other work situations (for example, schoolwork).

The end product is a disciplined young person who can work and save. For other teenagers, of course, this line of development is broken off, or for some reason it never begins. Earnings are frittered away; the youth drops out, or loses his focus, or slackens his efforts. The only hypothesis I have to offer about the successful development of this save-for-school pattern is that the longer it continues, the stronger it becomes. The greater the personal investment (of years spent working, saving, and studying), the more intense the motivation to persevere into a profession, and the stronger the disciplined habits.

4. A final category of lessons in teenagers' jobs involves social relations with the boss, customers, and fellow workers. The teenager has to adjust to a different kind of social situation, with somewhat different rules than he is used to. A series of summer jobs can help teach a youth to get along, socially, in nonschool, mixed-age, working-class social milieux. He may be put in situations where he is cheated and taken advantage of; he is at least given the opportunity to learn to fight for his rights and take care of himself.

"A few of my paper route customers tried to cheat me. They would say, 'I paid you last week.' I would say, 'All right,' and go on, even though I had the ticket which proved they hadn't paid me. I was afraid to say, 'Then why do I have this ticket, if you already paid?' "

Ron then went on to recount his subsequent jobs: dishwasher, tobacco picker, grounds-maintenance worker, herbicide sprayer, a factory worker, truck driver at Camp Bordon (Ontario), and finally his series of computer jobs.

In later instances of injustice, he no longer meekly submitted. His boss at Camp Borden did not think off-base kids should get the summer jobs, and he laid Ron off. Ron went to a government office, investigated the regulations, and found out that there was a rule against laying off students. He confronted the boss with this rule. The boss threatened him: "You'll never get another job at Camp Borden." Ron went over the boss's head and got himself rehired. The boss was incredulous.

Ron (at age twenty-four) is reputed to be a tough, shrewd person who is the favorite of his supervisor and is doing well in a government career; who can plan, save his money, fight for his rights; and who is admirably equipped to take care of himself. Assuming there is some truth to this image of Ron, it must be the end product of a line of development in which job incidents like this played a part.

Ron also learned to be dishonest himself, when he thought the occasion called for it. In talking about job hunting, he describes "making up sob stories" for the Canada Manpower counselor; once or twice he thinks this got results.

TRAVEL

Travel is another way to learn to manage one's own affairs. Some of the case studies, and my own recollections, suggest that children tend to take a spurt in maturity when they leave home. Summer camp often provides the earliest experience of this sort. In their late teens, youths sometimes go away for summer jobs; or they travel on school tours and on exchange programs (going to live with another family). They may also travel on their own, unsupervised. Long-distance hitchhiking is popular among my Dalhousie University students. They hitchhike back and forth across Canada; less frequently, I think, they venture down into the United States. Some of my students have also traveled, unsupervised, in foreign countries — doing it on a shoestring.

Hitchhiking and world traveling (without supervision) represent the most educational forms of travel, I think. They must be more dangerous too, although this is hard to calculate. None of my student hitchhikers had any serious trouble, not even the girls. Probably Canada is safer than the United States. As far as world-travelling is concerned, I think the main risk is getting sick from eating the food and drinking the water.

The most difficult and demanding form of travel must be hitchhiking — by yourself, with no companion — and with little money. Then you have to appeal to strangers for rides, and at every stop you are forced to go to strangers for occasional work, food, lodging sometimes, sociability, and things to do. People who have done this say, "This is the way you really get to know a country." Slightly lower on the traveling-difficulty scale are hitchhikers who travel with companions (the demands on one's self-reliance are less), and certain travelers by bus and even by car, who still must hustle and cope daily. (I am thinking here of low-budget travelers in exotic parts of the world: Mexico, Turkey, North Africa, etc.) Still lower on the difficulty scale is travel by car or by plane, in which money protects you from all this. You do not have to appeal to strangers, hustle for rides, food, lodging, or jobs. The students call this "the middle-class trip." Also low on the scale is supervised travel: with a school tour or traveling to a camp or to live with another family. The lowest point, the easiest and least demanding, is traveling with one's own parents.

It goes without saying that leaving home and traveling helps one learn to manage one's own affairs. It must promote personal growth and maturity in more ways than this. A hypothesis: The more radical the means of traveling, the more severe the demands for coping and using one's wits and being self-reliant — the greater its educational value.

CONCLUSION, AND A NOTE ON ANTICIPATING RISKS

Some impressive young people have furnished the material for this *Managing Affairs* chapter. There were the officeholders and managers, the conscientious volunteer workers who were offered managerial careers. I mentioned the cases of Babette, Irv, Jean, and Dave. I could have cited others. Two of my young managers have done more things, held more offices, and have more impressive résumés, than Babette, Irv, Jean and Dave.

Some of the hitchhikers and world travelers have had amazing careers. Roy started hitchhiking when he was eight. At eighteen, he had gone back and forth across Canada five and one-half times. Jerry hitchhiked to Mexico when he was fifteen. Later, he took off for Alaska, wearing sneakers with two dollars in his pocket. I know other hitchhiking youths who can match the records of Jerry and Roy.

Also there was Judy who was left alone, parentless (with her brothers) at age five and managed to survive in the big city, who learned to be self-reliant a full ten years "too soon." And there was Averill who managed the family store after her parents died.

These young people exemplify different lines of development — different styles of gaining experience and managing affairs. As the careers unfold there are changes, breaks in the sequence, surprises. Judy was forced to become less self-reliant at age nine. Irv opted out of his career as a result of a conversion to primal therapy. Jean also gave up her managerial career. Jerry is trying to settle down and put his life of adventure behind him, to study to be a schoolteacher. As their lives unfold, undoubtedly the surprises will continue.

Along with the changes and breaks in the careers, there is also a strain toward consistency. The cope-by-organizing people, who zip through a crowded schedule by means of superefficiency, seem to have established this style in their childhoods, when they were overloaded with work in their homes. Then they became even busier in high school, taking on offices and projects, continuing to overload themselves, and managing by means of efficient organization.

The enterprisers, the young people who develop a venturesome and innovative style and crowd their lives with rich experience — these people may shift their interests, but it seems that once the style becomes established it tends to continue too.

For the former officeholders and adventurers who claim to have put aside their earlier careers: what they learned must stay with them, resources available for future use.

The people I have talked about have done much in their

short lives. Other youths in my sample have done very little.
Still another type — the late starters — suddenly burst forth
and try to make up for lost time, after a quiet and sheltered
adolescence.

> Both Mike and Anne were slow developers. After a pro-
> tected childhood and adolescence, they both dropped out of
> college and lit out on their own — she to Europe with a
> boyfriend; he to Toronto. Dropping out and leaving home
> was an act of rebellion. For a while they did not communicate
> with their parents.
>
> Mike says he went through a period to trying to make up
> for lost time. He says he tried everything. I think that Anne
> must have done something like this too; and I know a
> number of other late-emancipated people who seem to have
> repeated this pattern.
>
> Things went well for a time. Then they ran into trouble.
> For both of them, their travels ended rather like the film
> *Going Down the Road;* they returned home with their tails
> between their legs. They went back to school, a bit beat-up,
> greatly experienced, and feeling very seasoned and matured.
> Whatever dangers and hard times they experienced seem not
> to have had lasting bad effects.

What does it matter if you go out into the world early or late;
if you do much or little in your teenage years; if you are precocious in this regard, or "held back," over-protected? Some
youth who are slow developers very likely make up for lost time
later on, in their early twenties (if not sooner).

There are about four different ways to answer this question.

• To repeat an argument I used earlier in the chapter: childhood experience and seasoning, early development, may improve a youth's judgment. He might be less apt to be taken in
by some dangerous influences, and might avoid a few mistakes.
This might be especially so if the early seasoning involves some
work and responsibility.

• The important thing is not so much early maturity or late
maturity, but putting together a good line of development and
avoiding a bad one. My hypothesis was: early seasoning with
responsibility can avoid some pitfalls.

• The exemplary cases I have cited — Judy, Irv, Babette,

Jean, Roy, and Jerry — illustrate some of the careers that can follow from an early start: rich lives, fun and adventures, work and interests; perhaps career preparation, and early maturity.

• People like Mike and Anne, who try their wings without benefit of prior seasoning, probably run greater risks. The danger of "bad turns" and mistakes would be greater, one would imagine:

If the person is chronologically younger (twelve instead of twenty), or inexperienced when he strikes out on his own;

If trying-your-wings is much influenced by rebellion or acting out a fictitious identity;

According to what the peer-influence is. It can be more or less dangerous or pernicious.

Some mistakes are harder to retrieve than are others. Some accidents and wrong turns have lasting influence, but most do not seem to have bad effects. Teenage drug users, radical revoluntionaries, and dropouts — it would be fascinating to follow them up and see how they have turned out. The sample of persons like this whom I know about is undoubtedly biased in favor of people who return to college and rejoin the "straight" world. For whatever it is worth, some of the dropouts have returned to school more focused and matured. The radical students are now leading quiet lives. A few are still in the Communist party, but most are not, and all went unpunished. The drug takers seem similarly unscathed.

On the other hand, Roy — after hitchhiking back and forth across Canada five and a half times — risked cold and exposure once too often. Now it appears that his health is damaged. Escapades do sometimes end in disaster. Then too, there are all the other wrong turns that are less conspicuous: unfortunate attitudes, beliefs that you cannot do this or that (because of traumatic and unsuccessful attempts), and lines of development that do *not* take place (such as school success and graduation from college).

When youth strike out on their own it may go well at first, and they are thrilled at their newfound freedom and proud of their grown-up functioning. Then potential dangers, complications, and other latent difficulties in their new situations make themselves felt. Examples are Mike, Anne, and similar *Going Down the Road* cases; Roy, whose health finally suffered from hitchhiking; a motorcyclist who eventually has an accident; a businessman, going into a new business venture, who cannot foresee the difficulties in the new situation and runs into trouble. A baby-sitting career is, to some extent, another illustration of this. One night's duty, baby-sitting, may be a quiet evening, with nothing to it. But over an entire career, some of the emergencies and trying situations which are latent in this job will in fact happen, and the baby-sitter will have to cope as best she can. The principle is: it takes awhile in a new situation, before you discover the complications, difficulties and dangers. A heedless youth may venture forth, ignorant of all this at first. (Erring in the opposite direction is the cautious person who lives in a rut, and no longer ventures at all.) The seasoned venturer anticipates complications, gets advice from people who have done it before, tries to draw on past experience, and recognizes obvious dangers.

Sooner or later experience will come, and if the youth is capable of learning from it, he will gain in wisdom. Hopefully no serious damage will be suffered in the process. How does one prepare a child for this? My only notion is (again): start him early and gradually on the road to autonomy; and give him responsibility, not just freedom to go off with his friends and have fun.

Chapter 13

ENTERPRISE

THE enterprisers are an elite group of fifteen or twenty people in the sample, who have led extraordinarily rich and active lives. Most of them are hobbyists in mechanical fields. They follow a pattern that was described in the *Mechanical* chapter: You work on the projects within an area of interest; this leads you into friendships in an interest group; these act back on your original interest; the circle of friendships widens; you get new interests; and one thing leads to another. The enterprisers represent the extreme of this pattern. They have many interests and a crowded social life. Their enthusiasm and pace of work is intense.

BOY INVENTORS

A few of my mechanical boys (as well as some grown men I have known) live creatively according to a pattern that goes something like this: The boy has a bright idea which involves making something. He does not know in detail how to do it or what he needs. He goes out to get the information and the material, and he tries to actualize his scheme. Original projects are combined with others that are easier and less innovative: making something from a kit or from plans in a magazine, following an already-established procedure. The bona fide invention attempts are rarely successful; but he keeps scheming, keeps trying.

Fred lives in a small Nova Scotia town. He began at age three, in the classic fashion of mechanical boys, taking apart a soldering gun. As he went through childhood he worked on bikes, appliances, a radio, his sister's motorcycle. He used to watch the mechanic work at the gas station, but he found this unsatisfying; you could only watch, you could not do it

184

yourself.

When Fred was fourteen he met his mechanical buddy, William Knickel. They shot ideas back and forth and inspired each other. Within a year they were building rockets and setting them off. They got interested in remote radio control, spent four hundred dollars on an airplane kit, built it, and wrecked the plane on its second flight. Then they made gasoline-engine air boats. He bought an old MG which now (four years later) he is still rebuilding and customizing. He got well-paying summer jobs (not easy to do) to pay for his expensive hobbies. The two boys went to a distant town, took flying lessons, and earned their pilots' licenses.

Most of their ideas never came to anything. They experimented with firecrackers and copper cylinders, and gave up the project as too dangerous. They did the same with hydrogen-filled cylinders (after making homemade hydrogen balloons). Fred's boy-scientist friend Chris gave him some plans and reading material on laser beams. He has wanted to adapt a laser beam to some original use. At his home are pieces of paper, diagrams, cut-out magazine articles — each representing a still-born scheme. These shade off into daydreams and idle speculations: combining hydrogen and oxygen to power an engine (he has read on the subject); ideas about storing the sun's energy; a design for a minicar and motor; salvaging materials from the town dump, inventing a tin-can crusher, a bottle-melter; a solar heating device; an underground home; and so on.

Fred says, "There are a lot of people like me who want to build things, but they can't because they don't have the plans, they don't know how." He has been stopped in numerous projects because he could never get the plans. He says when he was a little boy he wanted to be an inventor. Now he realizes how difficult this is, how much is involved in inventing something new and valuable. William has now gone off to sea. Fred is out of school and knocking around.

Since Fred lived in a small Nova Scotian town, not only did he have difficulty getting plans; he had little feedback on the feasibility of schemes, and a limited notion of what he *could* do. I think if he had grown up in a metropolitan center such as

Boston, with access to the expertise, information, and stores —
being able to join clubs and special interest groups — his
thinking would have taken less of a daydream quality. He
would have acquired city sophistication about what he could
do and how to go about doing it. He could have learned to use
the resources of the city in order to put projects together.
Another boy inventor, Paul Kay, developed in this more sophis-
ticated fashion.

Paul began his career when he was nine. His family had
moved to Lansing, Michigan, and he met Tom. They did at
least three things that Fred and William had done. They built
gas-powered airplanes and rockets, and they played with ideas
for doing something with laser beams. Together, they discovered various realms of technology, building things from kits
and plans, reading *Popular Mechanics* and talking about it,
and exchanging ideas. Although only little boys, they evidently
were more in touch with current developments than were Fred
and his friend in Nova Scotia. They build more things from
plans and kits, with no illusions about originality; and their
wild ideas and fantasies were probably on a higher order.

Paul's major interest, biology, was developing at this time.
The two boys did many things in the woods. They collected
insectivorous plants and did soil analyses to get the acid soil to
grow the plants. They located one boggy lake that had all the
plants except Venus' flytrap. They went through a period of
collecting fungi. They made ink out of mushrooms. Tom was
very interested in bees and in making honey for awhile, and
they kept bees in his backyard.

Paul and Tom worked on minibikes. They made go-carts.
Tom bought plans for a hover craft and actually made one.
They manufactured their own gunpowder and bombs. In the
woods, they build tree houses and forts out of branches. In the
neighborhood they build one very elaborate fort.

The boys would go out on the river in Tom's canoe; and they
would walk around in the woods, looking for things. "We
would talk all the time about ideas one or the other of us would
have. A lot of it was fantasy."

I interjected that to fantasize with another person, to do it together, is more comfortable. It validates your fantasies. It is not as if you are crazy. Also you can generate enthusiasm.

Paul said, "It is especially important to have a buddy when you are younger. Now I don't have one and I don't miss it."

This is not strictly true, but when Paul moved to Halifax at age twelve he never really found another Tom. His interests have continued to develop. They are too many to list, but they include elaborate cooking, a period of candy making, a period of serious skiing, and the mixing of potions in the basement. At fifteen, his main interest continues to be field biology.

Paul is an enterpriser. Not only does he initiate his own projects; he is unconstrained by social fear. Although his manner is quiet, refined, anything but "pushy," in the pursuit of his interests he could be termed socially aggressive. An example: Wishing to get out of gym class, he proposed a released-time arrangement to his high school. He would work in the Nova Scotia Museum in place of the gym class. Nothing like this had been done before, but he got permission to do it. At the museum he met Pierre, a botanist who was preparing to do a specimen-gathering survey of Nova Scotian plants. Paul got himself taken on as Pierre's unpaid assistant. They spent the summer in the field, and Paul learned a great deal of Pierre's craft.

Paul now likes to spend a day along the seacoast, gathering, identifying, and just being there, observing. He hitchhikes out after school, finds a place to sleep in a cabin or does chores at a home in return for a meal and a place to sleep, and he hikes along the coast the following morning. Usually he has no one to go with him; he does not mind going by himself.

Paul has put together a powerful combination: being a schemer of schemes — having bright ideas, being fired by enthusiasms, and setting about seriously to put them into practice — combined with being socially fearless, taking the initiative, going up to people and introducing himself.

The young enterprisers all appear to be this way (with the exception of Fred, who seems a bit shy). They are willing to take the initiative with other people. Their enthusiasms are genuine, and as a group they are extraordinarily attractive people, so they must have had much early encouragement in their social ventures. Their interests pushed them toward other hobbyists. They must usually have gotten positive responses, because of their enthusiasm and their attractiveness. And once the process got started, it must have become easier. (For one thing, their hobbies led them into social networks.)

BOY ENTREPRENEURS

With boy inventors the emphasis is on building things — creative mechanical work. They make tree houses, poison gas, and the like. If the emphasis is more on going out into the world to get information about how to do it, get material, and make novel arrangements with other people, this might be termed *entrepreneurship* instead. Fred is the classic inventor. Paul Kay spans both types. Pursuing his interests, he has operated in both ways.

The boy entrepreneurs are not especially interested in making money. What they want to do is to put their boyhood dreams into practice. Occasionally they succeed.

Bill Armstrong, like other car-crazed boys, wanted to build go-carts. At age twelve he got a paper route, saved twenty-five dollars, bought a motor, taught himself welding in the basement, and put it all together. He made a go-cart. But his welding career soon ended. He set the basement on fire and his father put a stop to it.

Paul Shea, at a similar age, watched a deep-sea diver (in an old-fashioned helmet and suit) at work. The ambition to be a diver stayed with him throughout his teens. He talked to divers, and read, and found out what was involved. He hatched the ambition to go into the underwater salvage business himself. By the time he entered the navy, he had accumulated equipment and he had made his start. Today he keeps in his kitchen the heavy brass diver's helmet which he himself made — a relic of that scheme.

Paul Shea,* along with Paul Mills (see below), has been my

---

*Paul Shea is a Boston psychologist. He lectures widely on preventive approaches to personal and organizational problems.

main theoretician on the subject of entrepreneurship and enterprise:

"The big thing about entrepreneurial activity is — you don't have it just dropped on you, like getting a model submarine, or going to a scheduled activity. You conceive what you want to make or what you want to do. Then you have to go around and inquire about the parts that are needed, how to get them, and learn how to make it from scrap parts or in some cheap way.

"I think entrepreneurship develops best in the absence of a lot of organized activities for kids. Maybe not being one of the gang helps.

"You can stay in expected roles that are prepared for you, or you can break the bonds of this and do things that are in psychic resonance with your inner self. If you get into the pattern of getting continual rewards for doing what everyone does, if you follow a socially prescribed scenario — then you don't develop creativity."

Paul's entrepreneur is one particular type, I think. He is thinking of himself as a boy and of a number of other people he has known and read about. Some of my enterprisers conform to his rules, and some do not. It is true that a number of the boys must have gone through a social outcast period; in one case particularly (Brent) this evidently had something to do with the innovative style he developed. However others did not. Several, like Paul Kay, did receive a great deal of help from their parents — books, lessons, equipment, advice, encouragement. Most of them have participated in organized activities — the YMCA, camps, school activities — and they made use of institutional facilities.

The enterprisers seem to be alike in these respects:

• They are socially venturesome.

• They have done a million things. Their short lives have been extraordinarily crowded. They got started on a process in which interests drew them into social encounters, and one thing led to another. Now (still in their youth) they are enormously experienced.

• They are very active. Some of them are probably, by constitution, high-energy types. But it is hard to be sure. An enthusiasm can energize; perhaps whirlwind activity can become a habit.

• Most are tinkerers. They are mechanical. They all seem to be determined and strong-minded, and each in his own way is a prodigious worker. In these respects, they resemble one profile of business entrepreneurs that has emerged from research.[1]

I would conjecture that the mechanical aptitude laid the groundwork for serious hobbying, which started the one-thing-leads-to-another process. The enterprisers are unusual (among hobbyists) for their original style, actualizing schemes, and for their unusual dynamism. But then nearly all of them are beautiful in their appearance and manner as well. They are all-round superior, it seems. Perhaps they have some real advantage in innate endowment.

Beyond this the similarities break down. Some did well in school, but most did badly. For some the label *inventor* fits; for others it does not. For several, mechanical work and hobbies are relatively unimportant.

Cases from the previous chapter could be included among the enterprisers. Managers such as Babette and Irv, and traveler-adventurers such as Jerry, are certainly enterprising by anyone's definition. They are very active and probably innovative.

Most of the enterprisers started out as mechanical hobbyists. But several, were officeholders, and several were traveler-adventures. (Most of the people finally did two of these things, and some did all three.) Any one of these career types can sometimes gather enough momentum — active plus innovative, one things leads to another — to produce an enterpriser.

Renaissance Man

Paul Mills, at twenty-six, must represent a grown-up stage of the career that Paul Kay has begun. Paul Kay's father first told me about him: that he was a teacher at the Free School, and that he had been an example to his son. He is constantly working to teach himself to do something new. At that time he

---

[1]Alexander Ross, "Anatomy of an Entrepreneur," *Quest*, January-February, 1975.

was taking his second sailing course (he did not own a boat), he was taking a course in Tai Chi, and he was constructing a hang glider in the basement. He was making the plane the hard way: fashioning the individual pieces from materials he had bought, working from diagrams. He had never before built or flown a glider. He expected to make his maiden flight that summer.

Paul was described as very disciplined and (unlike some of the younger boys) determined to finish the projects he started. He had been taking self-instruction, and courses, and learning skills like this for years. He could fix anything. He had spent the past summer working (for the fun of it) in Maine, helping a friend renovate an old house. His past ventures had taken him into Eastern philosophy and mystic quests, the straight business world, the hippie and drug scene, laboring jobs, tutoring the blind, youth work; he had done it all. At the center of his mechanical interests was woodworking, fine cabinet work; but his hobby ventures had been myriad.

I asked him how he did it. What was his formula; what were the crucial elements? How had he built his motivation; how did he keep it going? In trying to answer, Paul talked at times about himself, sometimes about other workmen, and also about other turned-on youths. ("This boy is about thirteen years old, really brilliant, and into electronics and other things. He came down to the school one day, but things moved much too slowly for him down there. He was in a constant frenzy of activity, creating.") These are some of the themes from his analysis, that pertain mostly to working on mechanical projects:

1. Bothering to understand the fundamentals of what you are working on, as opposed to just getting a result by copying, or reading the instructions: this, Paul thinks, is one thing that sets apart the problem solver and initiator.

2. High standards of quality and attention to detail; valuing high quality of workmanship. His rule is: the quality of a piece of work is roughly equal to the time spent on it. If you want better-quality work, spend more time on it.

3. *Nourishment* is his term for the rewards of work. Nourishment comes from working on a fairly challenging, exacting, difficult project, and doing it well — lavishing time and attention on it. You get nourishment from each little step in the

project. If the job is nourishing, you are enthusiastic and want to do it; it energizes you. Most journeyman workmen probably do not have this feeling. They cannot spend the necessary time to get high quality. In working in an eight-to-five routine, hurrying along, cutting corners and covering up mistakes, they lose any eagerness they may have had. The conditions of their employment are not conducive.

"After the job at Firestone [scraping paint] I promised myself I would never again do work that did not nourish me. . . . It's great when you finish something, and you can show it off and be proud of what you've done. But the daily progress you make, little problems that you overcome doing a job right; this gives just about as much satisfaction. . . . Men who do it at night as a hobby, who have a workshop in the basement — these are people who found their lifework too late. . . . Most carpenters in the building trades do not have this feeling, I don't think. They are in a routine, they have to go too fast. They are covering up mistakes and poor workmanship. But then every once in a while you meet a workingman who seems to have it. We visited a farmer in Prince Edward Island. He was so excited [about projects he was working on] he could hardly stay in the house long enough to eat."

What Paul is describing comes close to *flow* — the psychologist Csikszentmihalyi's term for being happily absorbed in an activity, wrapped up in what you are doing. Csikszentmihalyi[2] has observed this among painters, composers, surgeons, dancers, rock climbers, and chess players. Paul's own personal formula for keeping his interest fresh bears some similarity to Csikszentmihalyi's theory. Of course with Paul the emphasis is on mechanical work. Both make clear why most employment — doing work which has been given to you to do, in a job — violates the requirements of *flow* or *nourishment*.

4. "I need to be exploring frontiers, little personal frontiers. I have to make challenges for myself. As an example, I have never taken an engine completely apart. I know people have done it, and I can do it. Some day I will. I would get the

---

[2]Mihalyi Csikszentmihalyi, *Beyond Boredom and Anxiety* (San Francisco, Jossey-Bass, 1975).

instruction booklet, and I would do it.

"I like to work on a number of things at once, and have something on the back burner. Otherwise, I would be more apt to get tired of a job. I might have a frustrating design problem. It can work itself out as a result of subconscious work I do on it, if I can turn to something else for awhile."

His style seems to be to add a new project every few months. Some of them are exotic projects, such as the hang glider, a kayak he is making, and a particularly difficult problem in woodworking — a dictionary stand.

5. Paul thinks taking *risks* is necessary, to be really living and growing. Most of his examples were merely situations of social risk: facing possible embarrassment, not giving in to shyness, speaking out, and venturing into strange situations. ("You ask yourself: what is the worst that could happen to you here? Really, how close to death are you?") I think there are two points, here, that are important for an enterprising life-style.

First of all, the enterprisers are socially aggressive. They do not hesitate to go up to strangers — to fellow hobbyists, experts who can help them with a project, and people they meet in their travels. The nonenterprising life-style means settling into a comfortable rut, being too lazy or shy to make these social initiatives. The enterprisers either have little social fear, or they are courageous enough not to let shyness slow them down. There is probably a momentum effect, so that after a while this gets easier. Their contacts widen (and draw them into still new contacts), and their initiatives are often rewarded.

Paul also is willing to go out of his way, to really invest himself, for the sake of a new experience. He pays money, takes chances, inconveniences himself. For example, he had just returned from a brief and costly trip to Ottawa. He went to get Rolfed. (This is a very painful and "deep" kind of massage.) This theme appears in the stories of other enterprisers.

A hypothesis: One thing that separates the enterprisers from the rest of us is that they keep at it. Other people are occasionally venturesome and socially bold, but they do not follow it up. They withdraw into a rut again, or the conditions of their lives change, and they "forget" how to do it. With the enterprisers, the process — one thing leads to another — takes hold and continues. This may be one reason why mechanically based hobbies figure importantly in most of their lives. The hobbies make them join interest groups. This leads into (a) a widening circle of contacts and (b) new interests. In other words, they are drawn into fresh encounters; the interest groups must make it easier.

(This contrast between enterprisers and the rest of us should not be overdrawn. They also have their ups and downs. In a number of their stories there are periods of depression and quiet interludes, as well as some failures and bad experiences.)

———

We will now look at four more of these people — Kent, Brent, Judy, and Lea. All of them were students at Dalhousie University in Halifax.

Kent

Kent's story has already been partly told. He grew up in the small town of New Glasgow. Then his family moved to the city. This caused them to grow apart. In New Glasgow they had lived in a country-style, big, old house. There were many chores to do. As Kent remembers it, he was always keen to help. He mowed the large lawn, fed the wood-burning furnace, helped his father and uncle with various mechanical and maintenance jobs in and around the house, and on his uncle's boat. He and his brother made toys and play equipment for themselves: bows and arrows, sleds, a wooden wheel for a tricycle, hockey sticks, an intercom system, Soap Box cars, a play house.

> "My parents were always pretty careful not to mention any projects they wanted to do around the house, for I upon hearing would often try my best to help them out, which sometimes almost ended in disaster. I heard Dad mention one day that if they got a new car he would have to make the

garage longer by building an extension on the end of it. So one Sunday instead of making dinner I decided to give Dad a head start. I managed to get the rear out of the garage, but I had seriously endangered the stability of the garage to the point where if they had not come home when they did, it would have fallen in on me.

"My basic life-style in New Glasgow was one of continuous total effort. . . . There was no time whatsoever for being bored."

When Kent was about twelve years old, the family left New Glasgow and moved to Halifax. In the city their family life changed; they stopped doing things together. His mother started working, and Kent fixed the suppers.

"I adopted the Daniel family around the corner. In a sense they adopted me, for as they said, I was always very polite, helpful and sensible. I also helped Donnie a lot with his school work . . . There were chores to do around the house, and there were lots of kids around. Even though I did spend a lot of time there I still went home before supper to get it on and clean up."

The weakening of the family may have been crucial for Kent's development as an enterpriser, because it helped free him from parental supervision. When they lived in New Glasgow, before his mother went to work:

"I did not have to think while at home, for Mom did that for me by notes, phone calls, and in person at night. Everything was planned, and how I hated that.

" . . . I grew independent at a very young age, which probably could have even started in New Glasgow. I cooked my own food, left when I wanted, went to school when I wanted, had money when I wanted it and was free during the day from a nagging mother — in person, that is. . . . My parents left us alone for the first time when I was in grade six and we made out really well. Brian was in high school then and we were pretty sensible.

Evidently Kent began on a good course of development (as a result of the early household work and responsibility training?), so he was "sensible" and "proved he could handle it" when his parents gave him freedom. However it happened, he got considerable autonomy when they moved to the city.

Weak parental supervision probably helped the enterprisers get started. Most (but not all) of the enterprisers seem to have this in their backgrounds. This makes sense. With less interference from parents, the youth's exploits and ventures would have more freedom to unfold. Also, we have cases like Judy. She had to fend for herself when she was a young child. This must have provided the foundation, the start, for her later enterprising career.

Kent's interests have spanned short-wave radio, sailing, skiing, traveling, youth work, crafts, and working on the house he bought on St. Margaret's Bay. To illustrate Kent's all-out style of endeavor, I will quote from his description of his leather work.

"A friend of mine started making leather goods as a hobby. I watched him work and ended up buying two belts. I found out where to get the leather and the tools. From that point on it just grew and grew. [He was sixteen.]

"I set up shop in the basement of my parents' flat. I had never really gotten into crafts before but I [got great satisfaction from doing high-quality work]. Some nights I worked until two or three in the morning. My business reached the point where my goods were selling themselves by word of mouth alone. [He made regular trips to New Brunswick to buy materials.]

"By the end of the first year I was making belts, hats, bags, shoulder bags, and odds and ends averaging about two hundred dollars à month worth of goods. I was also selling my goods through a boutique in Wolfville, but I did not like making goods without knowing the [eventual buyers].

[He describes how he made leather articles for people, on order, and he enunciates an old-fashioned code of superior craftsmanship.] "Then I showed [the customer] the [finished product] and it had to suit perfectly or I would not sell it to him.

"I guarantee everything and always tell people to return anything they might have problems with. I made money, and yet people were really happy to buy it."

He also began teaching leather work. He was offered several

leather shop jobs but he turned them down. He felt the mass production situation would kill the joy (and the quality) in the work.

> "I really liked working for myself. I could project my own values. . . . It was hard work at times and yet it was always fun. It's strange how an old basement can be converted into a haven by something as simple as a craft."

Like the other cases I have cited — Fred, Paul Kay, and Paul Mills — Kent's enthusiasm did not extend to school. The enterprise career is something that happens outside of school, in spite of school. In school one is "sleepy," to use Paul Mills' term.

BRENT

Brent grew up in a comfortable home in Edmonton, Alberta. He had few chores to do. He had no mechanical apprenticeship. Today he is a prodigious worker with very high standards. He seems to resemble his father, who is a dynamic entrepreneur with perfectionistic work standards. But Brent's development cannot be explained by reference to early modeling. His father was seldom home; he was traveling much of the time, and then he left home for good.

Brent describes himself as a rebellious "bad" child both at home and at school.

> "By four years of age I was terrorizing the neighborhood on my [bike] . . . so continued my infatuation with wheels, speed, and the increased freedom they could provide.
>
> "At five, my war with those trying to control me continued on a grand scale — during my very first day of school I was locked in the closet for screaming and throwing crayons at the teacher. I was bad and although I'm not particularly proud of it, I don't hardly regret any experience that I managed to scrape through.
>
> "I never spent much time with any group of kids; I was sort of an outcast. . . . I was teased, and I took it to heart. I became a real loner and made good times for myself. Many happy hours were spent chasing mice in the fields across the trans-Canada highway." [And he described his cardboard mouse catcher.]

Brent wandered the country on his bicycle, helped farmers with haying, got lost, spent one night in a culvert. When he was about nine the family moved to Dartmouth, Nova Scotia. He sees his perfectionistic work habits beginning at this time, in doing yard work. (This was described in Chapter 10.)

When Brent was twelve, the family moved back to Edmonton. He began to invent new (and risky) ways to have fun.

"In shop in grade seven I made strap-on spikes for my boots and I used them and a bunch of belts [like telephone linemen use] to allow me to climb tall trees that I could otherwise not have climbed. With this outfit I built a tree house nearly 30 feet in the air. . . . In shop that year I also made a simple makeshift gun that could propel an aluminum shot completely through a piece of half-inch plywood and take a big chip out of a cement wall (our garage). . . .

"I really liked to make things and my imagination and enthusiasm usually carried me away, so to speak. I made and introduced the first pair of 15-foot solid maple stilts in our rather stuck-up neighborhood. I used to get up on them from the roof of our split-level house, and I could easily walk over stop signs; kids rode under me on bikes, and car owners shook when I walked near their parked cars. It was a lot of fun. I guess I could have been looking for attention, but I sure enjoyed the thrill of it all."

He had worked at odd jobs for some years: yard work, a paper route, gopher hunting (with bow and arrow). At thirteen he started saving for a motorcycle. He worked as a dishwasher, and at a golf course, and he bought the bike.

"I made steel plates for the bottoms of my special riding boots. I used to go riding around on my bike, and when I placed my feet on the pavement I would leave a beautifully brilliant 'rooster tail' of sparks.

"I almost failed grade nine because of my "deplorable school attitude" and poor work habits. I was a hopeless case, and by now I was ready to believe it. In the meantime, though, I became almost totally involved in sports: track, football, baseball, golf, curling, skiing [at Jasper and Banff], cycling, swimming and diving, kite flying, and motorcycle riding. I loved trying everything . . . [later] some gymnastics, and I became gung ho on the sport of ski jumping."

He learned judo and karate, but he also learned to type. He typed school papers for his friends and for his sister and her friends, usually free of charge. At sixteen he ran away from home for the first time; he went to British Columbia in search of his father.

He saved money for a bigger, faster motorcycle. He made (and kept) a vow never to drink or smoke. He bought his first old car and reconverted the trunk into a rumble seat so he could carry up to fourteen passengers. He left home for the second time and knocked around British Columbia.

"... landed a job renting and fixing paddle boats and rowboats that Penticton Water Sports Ltd. rented to the tourists on the shore of the lake.

"Here I learned *how not to* and *how to* fiberglass boats; in the meantime I improved my water skiing and scuba diving that I had picked up in high school. I slept in my tent most of the time, but I occasionally dug myself into the sand or stayed in the back of one of the towboats on the nice, warm summer nights. My three and one-half months of cooking over a fire helped me to lose about twenty extra pounds, and it also prompted me to become a much less picky eater. I'll eat almost anything now. . . . I sometimes moonlighted by picking fruit in the valley, and I spent the winter working in the grocery store." [The next summer he taught water skiing.]

After this, Brent traveled across the country to rejoin his father in Nova Scotia. From here on, his life seems to have become more crowded, and his period of work overload begins. He held down four fairly responsible jobs in his father's businesses — simultaneously, "seven days a week." He took up sky diving. And he ran a businessman's fitness class at the YMCA.

"At the Y, I met a girl whose father works in the Department of Education. They talked me into living with them while I gave grade twelve another crack. I walked into a tightly knit family of nine with a little guy of one and a half years old, a slightly older sister, and a handicapped boy of twelve who was almost as big as I was. . . .

"During that year, my twentieth, I became overloaded with

various activities, as is customary. I had a normal grade twelve load of classes and took Geology at night school out of interest. At the Y, I ran the fitness class in return for membership; lifeguarded and helped with the swim program; became involved with a program for the mentally retarded; and was an active member of the leadership group. On Tuesdays and Thursdays, I helped to run a Cub Scout program in St. Paul's Church in Dartmouth. My time was spread a little thin, and I had to learn to cope with it. I did this by learning to organize my time and activities very well. The fact that I seemed to always function best when under pressure allowed me to complete my homework (for a change) and this reversal . . . provided me with a graduation with honors. Wouldn't my old teacher just die laughing.

"[With the little boy] we became very close. I learned to dress, change, and bathe him. I would play with him endlessly and read to him at night. . . . If he had bad dreams at night, I would often sit and comfort him.

"During that eventful year [in that home], I did the usual chores. . . . The kitchen was a constant mess; there were piles of dirty dishes since they had very little counter space and they were done once a day. It was not unusual to find them piled high on the floor, so you had to watch your step as the day ended. Since I was used to the 'clean, neat, and tidy' atmosphere, it took a little getting used to. I turned out to be the one who spent at least an hour a night doing the dishes and cleaning up the kitchen. I didn't really mind, though. I ended up with a 'good, dependable' reputation in working with and controlling little kids. That is another side of me that hadn't emerged before (and might not again if Judy and I play our cards right)."

The next year, Brent entered Dalhousie University in Physical Education. He has had other jobs; more work with the Y and with the handicapped; new hobbies (furniture refinishing, horseback riding, farming with his father, dancing in shows); more tours on his motorcycle; and more sports (mainly gymnastics and cross-country running).

And Brent met Judy. ("He captured my heart with his motorcycle.")

"Every weekend I drove my bike 600 miles to see Judy and

every now and then she came back with me and worked around the farm. I've never seen a girl who could work so long and hard as she did and does. She is something else. We were married last July thirty-first, and we went camping in a pup tent for a couple weeks on Prince Edward Island."

This summer they are touring the country on a motorcycle.

JUDY AND LEA

Judy was an early developer. When she was kindergarten age, she survived a Toronto winter without mother or father (previous chapter). At twelve she taught dancing, gymnastics and swimming at the Sydney, Nova Scotia, YMCA. By thirteen she was performing on television and giving talks and demonstrations to promote Y programs. She also held two very demanding camp counselor jobs. She lied about her age to get these jobs. But she seemed so mature — and actually was so experienced — that people assumed she was years older. At fourteen, she had an adventured-filled summer in Boston (flying in from Cape Breton, sitting in Logan Airport, looking at the want ads in the *Boston Globe,* finding a job, and going on from there.) In her own way, she is almost as spectacular as her husband Brent.

The final case is Lea, who says about herself:

"I would describe myself as fairly industrious, an organizer of sorts, and a 'finisher.' I am a whiz at finding all kinds of things to do and at times drive myself crazy because I have to be continually doing something. Relaxing, to me, means sewing or reading directions on how to make something."

As a little girl she helped with gardening and housework, copied after her mechanical father, and became an ardent fixer. She also learned various household arts.

When Lea was ten her mother died. She says the result was "instant maturity." Lea tried to take her mother's place and do her work. Since then she has had a career in art (winning a scholarship to the Nova Scotia College of Art while in grade six), teaching art and working with children (including several summers as a Head Start worker and team leader), and a career as a pretty girl (she has modeled, off and on, since grade ten).

Like Judy and the other enterprisers, Lea's social contacts are extensive. Her networks center in Halifax, her home town. Her personal resources are varied. She has done, and could do, a variety of things. The problem of career choice is simply a matter of choosing one.

CONCLUSION

These seem to be the core traits of the enterprisers:

1. The habit of enterprise: the nerve and confidence to venture (in a particular area of activity), and some past knowledge of how to start, from having done it before.

2. "Continuous total effort" (as Kent says) — enthusiasm, intense activity.

3. They are workers on projects, in areas of interest. Most are mechanical, problem solvers.

4. They are disciplined workers with high standards. (There are several borderline cases and possible exceptions here.)

5. Then there is the "career" aspect — getting drawn into an area of interest, one project leading to the next, and the social side of the interests — as described in the *Mechanical* chapter.

How did they get that way? What are the antecedents?

First of all, we have Paul Shea's and Paul Mills' own personal formulas, which differ; enterprise itself is not a unitary trait.

We can roughly identify the process that has to be set in motion (the above points, especially points one and five).

Mechanical work, leading to serious involvement in hobbies, seems to have been the background of most of the enterprise careers.

Freedom from parental interference, teenage autonomy, was probably helpful.

Then we have suggestions of other causes in individual cases: family responsibility taken on early in life; early work training, early self-maintenance training; and perhaps superior endowment (energy level and personal beauty).

The enterprisers seized on various resources in their communities; the YMCA (Brent and Judy), the leatherwork hobby complex of Halifax (Kent), Jewish organizations (Irv), Boston's resources of information and expertise (Paul Shea), the Nova Scotia Museum (Paul Kay). Only one of them seems to have been thwarted in his development, because his community did not offer enough (Fred).

Challenging situations figured prominently in their careers. Lea tried to take her mother's place at age ten; later, as a teenager, she led Head Start teams into impoverished little communities. Judy, at age five and without parents, survived a winter in Toronto. At twelve she was teaching for the Y and performing on TV; and she went on to camp counseling jobs. Brent teaches himself one skill after another: judo, karate, sky diving, scuba, fiberglass boat building, typing, dance routines, and more sports, along with countless dangerous escapades. The boy inventors and entrepreneurs tackle new projects and take up fresh hobbies. Part of Paul Mills' enterprise formula was: exploring personal frontiers.

The challenging situations test them. The challenges bring out a better effort, require more in the way of self-discipline or nerve. Rising to challenges like this, they learn lessons in self-management; they grow, and add to their sense of competence.

Risk is involved in some of these challenges. Sometimes it turns out badly, as it evidently did when Lea tried to take her mother's place. The live-dangerously youths, like Brent, actually risk life and limb.

In less dangerous challenge situations — the sort that we all must face sometimes — a person may risk a devastating failure that closes off a line of development. The lessons learned from these are "I can't do that" or "I'll never try that again." I am thinking of university students in difficult programs that prove to be too much for them; people who move up to challenging jobs that they cannot handle (as with myself, in a brief and disastrous try at an administrative job); and travelers like Mike and Ann in the last chapter, who "go home with their tails between their legs."

Chapter 14

PREPARATION FOR
12,489 LIFE SITUATIONS

THE enterprisers have done so much; they seem well equipped for the future. They know how to get into things, have fun, and lead rich lives. They are workers. Thrust into a situation, they seem likely to make the best of it — cope, enjoy, and give a good account of themselves. Career choice does not look like a serious problem for them; their great resources give them flexibility and freedom of choice. One has the feeling that they could change their minds, or seize a sudden opportunity, and do very well wherever they found themselves.

Managers such as Babette, Irv, and Jean, and mechanical hobbyists such as Harry: the same might be said for them.

Other youths seem solidly prepared in some limited area. They do not have the skills and broad preparation of the enterprisers. They seem like good, viable people, but they will probably do less. And they seem less well prepared for life's surprises and disasters; they have fewer resources on which to draw. These people show a good line of development in some one area. I am thinking, here, of good students I have known, who had never done much outside school; also sweet, nurturant girls who have taken care of children and who are ready to be mothers.

Then, toward the bottom of the scale, I know other young people whose preparation for life is pathetic. Their resources are meager.

> Joy is perhaps the most resourceless student I have known. She is blind. She does get people to help her; this seems to be her only skill. She is a poor student, but she manages to stay in college. She is unattractive, dirty, and smelly. She seems to have no friends. She has no real career plan, just some wild fantasies. What will become of her?

Bill is not so disadvantaged as Joy. In some ways he seems a fairly ordinary college student, but he cannot spell. He failed school once. When he tells the story of his life, he lists a series of failure experiences. He says he is lazy. He has done little, had little in the way of interests. And he sits in class with a dreamy, bemused expression on his face.

George is a high school student who has probably spent most of his life sitting listlessly — in school, in front of the TV set, and just sitting. He never had a real hobby. He never competed in sports. He is shy. In school work, things have gone from bad to worse. Bored and lazy, he has now fallen behind in some subjects, such as math. He sits and daydreams and dislikes it. He has had two menial jobs. Surprisingly, he did very well in them. As a manual laborer, he worked like a strong man. He has proved he can hold a job. But beyond that, what will happen to him?

There are huge differences between young people — between Joy at one end of the scale and Brent and Judy at the other. For some, you can tote up many strengths:

Lea is a pretty girl. She can trade on her good looks and be a model. She is artistic: She can teach art or be a designer. She writes well. She can work with children. She has the habit of enterprise. She has extensive social contacts in her home town. She is even a lady mechanic. The list goes on.

For other people, going over the same areas, you find deficiencies instead:

Joy is unattractive, untalented, a bad student, inexperienced in the world of work. She has no friends. She is enterprising only in getting people to help her cross the street, climb the stairs, find her way in and out of buildings, and do her schoolwork. She is not even sighted.

Young people's preparation for life can be viewed in another way. Rather than adding up strengths and deficiencies in various areas of functioning, one can try to imagine all the situations they will be put in: 12,489 situations? That is fanciful, of course; but it would be some huge number.

There are many situations they will *have* to cope with — there is no escaping them. There are other things that are optional. They can be avoided if one wishes. The situations can be charted into areas or sectors: child care; family relations; sex; housework; cooking; dirt and disorder; camping out and roughing it; schoolwork; jobs; dealing with a big city; driving; fights, conflicts, and standing up for oneself; operating within bureaucracies, dealing with red tape, filling out forms; book-keeping and office work; committees and meetings; dancing; parties; situations where one might be shy and awkward; travel; learning languages; writing papers; photography; diving, tennis, skiing, other sports; mechanical repairs; being in physical pain (and so on).

This is a way of thinking about human happiness and adjustment. Rather than trying to judge it overall, you look at all the situations in which you are placed. You do well in some and badly in others. You are happy in some situations and unhappy in others.

Also, it is a way of thinking about human potential. Picture a person — such as yourself — and try to imagine his entire life space. Some situations, people, activities, are congenial; others are uncongenial, and you try to avoid them. The person is hedged by certain aversions, inhibitions, "can't stand this's" and "can't do that's." Psychological scars from the past, aversive learning, have closed off various areas. One may be shy at parties, unable to dance, mechanically inept, or repelled by dirty diapers — and that's that; there is not much one can do about it. On the other hand, skills and confidence gained from past experience may enable one to do certain other things: run a meeting, manage an office, write a paper, and so on.

I think that when people try new things, they tend to venture into areas that are similar to things they can already do. Skills you already have, things you are good at, situations you are comfortable with — these are your stepping-stones to new experience. The enterprisers' careers illustrate this. They kept their momentum; one thing led to another.

Farm work, child care, mechanical work, office holding, serious hobbies — these prepare young people to do various other things (making allowance for some cases of failure and aversive learning). Past experience in these makes them skilled and comfortable in certain situations. Not only could they handle various jobs that are thrust upon them; they will also have the capacity to go on and seek certain new experiences.

I will give two examples — a good example and a horrible example.

The good case is Lorraine, whom I described at the beginning of the *Farms* chapter. Lorraine's mother goes through the day, does her work, takes care of her family, and serenely handles the many tasks and emergencies that come her way. Lorraine is her lieutenant. She minds the smaller children. She helps out in the kitchen, and works on farm tasks. She goes down the road and helps her grandmother.

Lorraine appears to be copying after her mother. She seems nurturant toward the little ones, responsible, helpful. She is apprenticing to farmwife work and she has a good model to copy. I would make these predictions about what sort of woman Lorraine will become:

She will be well prepared for motherhood and for doing numerous farm tasks. She has been hardened so as not to mind a variety of discomforts, as she has been hardened to cold and to arduous work. Her mother's style is to cope with emergencies cheerfully and serenely. Lorraine shows this tendency too. She would be a good camper, farmwife, and mother — unflustered by any mess.

Not only will she perform well in these situations; also (I would predict) she would not complain. The people around her will be buoyed up by her good spirits, rather than dragged down by her complaints and personal problems. On work teams that resemble her farm family, she will be a willing and cooperative worker.

Lorraine is an example of a child who is being prepared for the future — just in certain areas, not in others — by the work she is doing now.

The horrible example is myself. As a child, I went to school and played sports: baseball in the summer, football in the fall, basketball in the winter. These were interspersed with other sports as I got older — Ping-Pong, tennis, and finally golf. My friends and I — we did little else. We played the sports. We read about them in the sports page of the newspaper. We listened to games on the radio; we went to see the high school teams play. We worked at getting better, and we emulated the sports heroes. What I looked forward to (secretly) was to wear one of those uniforms, hear the crowd's roar, and be a football hero myself.

The parents who permitted all this useless activity had various rationalizations. It was good for the boys; it was character building; it taught one to be a good loser; it taught boys to be "fighters," fierce competitors; it taught teamwork; it toughened boys, gave them "hard knocks." Who knows? Perhaps the sports were not entirely useless. But one thing is evident. Since I spent my free time playing sports, I was *not* doing other things, such as mechanical work, or caring for a baby, or helping with the housework, or getting interested in a hobby. Since we were so focused on becoming football heroes, we did not emulate (or even notice) other grown-up role models.

When I entered the army, at age eighteen, they put me to work as a typist. That was the one skill I possessed that the army could use.

I always did well in school — my mother got me off to a good start — and I developed into a reader and a writer. This led me into a career as a professor. It is fortunate that I can do this. Otherwise, I am hedged and limited by various *can'ts*. For some reason — perhaps it was unfortunate learning in early childhood — certain areas were closed off. Also, I was not getting Lorraine's preparation (nor was I the enterprisers', or the officeholders', or the serious hobbyists'.) I was trained to be intolerant of dirt and disorder. Changing a dirty diaper? Horror of horrors! When my turn for parenthood came, I suffered through the diaper stage as best I could, but it was a trial for everyone.

Most of us will be confronted, sooner or later, by that baby who needs his diapers changed, as we will by a flat tire, a court summons, an income tax return, innumerable other situations in which we will have to perform as best we can. How well we acquit ourselves depends on how well we are prepared. Just what goes into that preparation is rather mysterious, to be sure. But the youthful careers I have been describing — of farm children, little mothers, mechanical boys, serious hobbyists, managers, enterprisers — these look like part of the answer. They prepare for certain parts of one's future.

EVALUATING CHILDREN'S ACTIVITIES

Another way of answering the question — how worthwhile are various childhood activities as preparation for the future — is to do a sort of task analysis. Lorraine's case could be taken as an example — the various benefits she seems to be getting from her work around the farm. As for my years of baseball, basketball, and football, I would give them a rating of zero: not harmful, but not helpful either. Learning to type, which my mother forced me to do one summer, was enormously helpful. Typing is a strategic skill that came in handy many times.

One can ask of an activity, what skills are being learned? Are these skills of any use? Are they applicable to future situations? Do they open any doors? One can further ask, what are the "lessons" being learned? Is there transferrable experience that the child is picking up? Finally, what traits are being fostered? (As with the responsibility training, hardening, and training in helpfulness that Lorraine appears to be getting.)

An example is my older son's paper route. Going on his route with him at 6 AM, I decided it was fairly limited as a learning experience. He learned a couple of specialized skills — folding the newspapers and throwing them onto porches — which were of no use once he left that job. He had to remember his route, be on time, and deliver the paper unfailingly, every day. Once he had proved to himself that he could be a reliable paperboy, the job had little more to offer him. Perhaps, over time, transactions with route manager, substitute, and customers may have provided an occasional lesson.

I think most paid jobs that teenagers get are like this. The jobs' learning potential is used up rather quickly.

Work that is less routinized has more "in" it to be learned. Lorraine, for example, did some routine chores, but she had many different kinds of jobs to do. And as she grew older, she received more grown-up responsibilities. It added up to rich diversity — much "there" to be learned — some skills and lessons that could be applied later in life, and the molding of her character.

The same could be said for the mechanical hobbyists: fixing and building, problem solving, moving on from one project to the next. Their work is not a closed routine. It is open ended, progressive, a career. There is much to be learned; and there are useful applications to later life (listed at the end of the *Mechanical* chapter).

The managers' careers also have this open-ended quality.

The mother's helpers — doing child care and housework — do experience some boring routine, but they also graduate to more grown-up responsibilities as they grow older. And their early work in their own homes is followed by more variety when they got older; they baby-sit in other homes. They acquire certain useful skills, learn various lessons, and tend to develop into helpful and responsible persons.

———

Our children spend their time at school and at play — in little recreations. They learn games and sports, shuffleboard, Ping-Pong, and Monopoly®. If one evaluates these recreations as to what their application might be in later life, most of them are trivial. This is all right; children have a lot of time. But it is good to keep in mind the activities that *do* have payoffs — typing, mechanical repairs, baby-sitting, and the rest. These can be completely crowded out by other things.

INDEX